FINDING HOPE

IN CRAZY TIMES

Daily Stories
of Hearing God

D1554333

ANDY MASON

Finding hope is essential to a successful life. In these pages you'll find a guide who has a string of successes finding exactly what you are looking for. Andy Mason is a hope seeking missile! He has a beautiful attitude in any challenge he faces. I've heard him say "just keep walking" a thousand times. His tenacity to believe the best and to trust God will inspire you to do the same. I highly recommend you allow Andy to guide you in Finding Hope!

DANNY SILK
President of Loving on Purpose
Author of *Keep Your Love On and Culture of Honor*

Life is a wild and crazy adventure, and if you've found yourself in the midst of challenging times, you will surely find your own story within these pages. More importantly you'll find encouragement and will encounter the goodness of an extravagantly loving God.

SHAE BYNES
Founder of Kingdom Driven Entrepreneur, Atlanta, GA
Author of *Grace Over Grind: How Grace Will Take Your Business Where Grinding Can't*

Andy Mason has given us a great gift. In this book, he shares the accumulated spiritual wisdom gained through years of allowing God to lead him through life's trials and tests. Every page I read encourages me. I know it will encourage you too."

RAY EDWARDS
International Speaker and Author of *How to Write Copy that Sells*

Within the pages of this book are simple, yet incredibly profound stories that not only made scripture come alive for me, but Andy's practical testimonies opened up new caverns of hope in my heart to see and hear the Father in a fresh way for my own life. The depth of Andy's relationship with God is evident, and these daily devotional are almost like a personal invitation into his sacred secret place with the Lord, showing us how we too can have a deep well with our Beloved Jesus. This book will surely help you take your eyes off the size of the challenge you may be facing, and put them back on His goodness, His kindness, and His faithfulness to make us the head and not the tail every situation.

CARLA PRATICO
Founder of She Roars
President of branding firm Polus Digital, Inc., New York, NY

Andy Mason is one of the most positive people that I have ever met; he is also very inquisitive, searching for new experience and understanding as he walks the path of life. In addition, he lives a life of encouragement and stimulation towards other people on a daily basis. My friendship with Andy has led me to believe that one of the most important tools he has utilized in developing such a lifestyle is the ability to keep growing in hope no matter what the circumstance. He is not afraid to trust God when it looks risky, and has endured hardships with remarkable faith. There is a Bible verse that summarizes the journey of Andy's life: Romans 15:13 "I pray that God, the source of hope, will fill you completely with joy and peace because you trust in him. Then you will overflow with confident hope through the power of the Holy Spirit." Andy overflows with hope and this book can help you on that journey.

DR PETE CARTER
Founder of Heaven in Healthcare and Director of Eastgate Church, England Author of Unwrapping Lazarus

There are only a handful of people who I can say, "this person changed my life." Andy Mason is one of those people. I'll never forget the moment that I heard Andy share the life transforming insight that the promptings, inspiration and things I felt led to do and/or say were "PROBABLY God, but that they MIGHT be me." Prior to this insight, I had lived according to the belief that it was "PROBABLY me, and that it only MIGHT be God." Since experiencing this paradigm shift for myself, I've learned that God has ALWAYS been talking directly to me (and through me). For the past several months of my life, I've experienced more peace, joy, love and abundance than I ever dreamed possible before. I credit the insight, that "It's PROBABLY God, but it MIGHT be me," for the fact that I finally know how to experience a life where I can "be anxious about nothing." In the pages of this book you will find the same transforming insights for yourself.

CLIFF RAVENSCRAFT
Business Mentor, Life Coach and Motivational Speaker

Finding Hope in Crazy Times is a treasure, filled with truth and wisdom from Andy and Janine's life of stepping out, and into all God has invited them and their family to experience. By sharing personal stories with candor and wisdom, Andy opens the door for us to grow in faith that God is truly with us in every circumstance and season we encounter. Each story, Scripture, prayer and application gives us practical ways to connect more deeply with the hope found in Jesus, and to "taste and see that the Lord is good" for ourselves. I highly recommend this book, whether your life feels crazy or not.

CANDICE KLOPFENSTEIN
Artist, Chicago, IL

Andy Mason has a brilliant book with *Finding Hope in Crazy Times*. From one simple, practical installment to the next, Andy captures powerful life and leadership insights that anyone can apply. Readers who internalize one installment a day, in the midst of their crazy schedules, will have a substantially saner life within just a year. I'll be one of those readers!

CHUCK PROUDFIT
Founder and President of At Work on Purpose, Cincinnati, OH

Andy has such a gift for releasing freedom, imparting hope and helping people to dream with God again. This book is packed with everyday stories of Andy's supernatural life journey with God in work, ministry and family. His disarmingly-relatable story-telling style is embedded in biblical context and coupled with deep questions for reflection, suggested activities and powerful prayers that will encourage and activate you into all God has promised.

BRENDON KNOTT, PHD.
Associate Professor in Sport Management, Cape Peninsula University of Technology, South Africa

As a leader and communicator, Andy offers hope to all in need. His writing style ignited faith in my heart. His use of stories created wonderful continuity that brought context in the midst of challenges. His conviction that God is good and He wants favorable things taking place in your life, brought about conviction that all things *are* possible for those who believe. The testimonies of hearing the voice of God in the midst of contention released confidence in my heart that God is near.

BOB PERRY
Director, Integrative Prayer Solutions, Nashville, TN

As I read through the pages of *Finding Hope in Crazy Times*, I could sense in the words experience and growth, which come from taking time to hear God and valuing what He has spoken. I read one chapter a day and then meditated, prayed, worshiped and journaled around it. God spoke to me in a very clear and personal way every day. Andy's vulnerability has always been an inspiration and has always challenged me to go deeper and further in my personal walk with God. As a result, those around him are inspired to walk closer with God bringing hope to many, in many places of the world. This book gives light, hope and boldness to continue the journey keeping a sense of awe and expectation to what is ahead.

MAGNOLIA DE GUDIEL
Director of Zona Cero and Supernatural Business Transformation, Guatemala

Finding Hope in Crazy Times is a God-send in our current world. Andy's openness and honesty of his family's calling and challenges, coupled with testimonies of God's miraculous breakthroughs, will inspire you to press on and thrive in your calling and walk with the Lord. This book is a powerful tool not just for the business realm, but also for all of life. I have personally been renewed in my desire to fight the good fight using Scripture and the words the Lord has spoken to me, and I know you will too. Andy helps us to see that our lives are more significant than we think, and that together with the Lord and one another we can accomplish incredible things.

COLIN WALKER
Consultant Humanitarian Trainer, South Africa

From my first meeting with Andy, I knew he had met with God and carries a powerful story of promise. It became even more prevalent when I met his kids…without knowing ANYTHING about me, my family or my business, his teenage son began to declare God's promises over me for the year ahead with CRAZY accuracy and precision, all with the same authority his dad carried. You know you are witnessing something special when the same power and authority that mom and dad carry transfers over to the kids in such a special way. Let Andy and Janine's stories of God's promises for their family be a building block of faith for your own. Where you have need, borrow some of their faith to see God move in amazing ways to empower you to write your own stories of God's promises to share with the world.

LEIGH ARCHER
Chief Operating Officer, KeyCity Capital, Colorado

Finding Hope in Crazy Times, Daily Stories of Hearing God

© 2019 Andy Mason
All rights reserved

Cover design by Nick Wallace, Red Dove Design
Formatting by Nick Wallace, Red Dove Design
Authors photo by Josh Tate

All scripture quotations unless otherwise indicated,
are taken from the New King James Version.
Copyright ©1982, Thomas Nelson Inc.
All rights reserved.

ISBN: 9781670162274

To order more books or resources contact us at AndyandJanine.com

CONTENTS

ACKNOWLEDGMENTS

Thank you to the team and friends around me who have been a source of comradery, strength and encouragement on this journey. Namely, thanks to Steve, Jesse, Chris and Eric with whom I get to regularly and consistently share life – the ups and the downs.

Thanks to Darrel and Mary Miller who helped underwrite this book project and have been a wonderful part of our crazy house story. Thanks also to Tim and Jaime Smith for helping this project launch!

Janine, thank you for being my best friend and not letting go as we have walked through this crazy time together. Thank you for loving me enough to speak the truth and loving me in spite of my delayed responses to what God has been trying to teach me. Thanks for taking this work and turning into something beautiful that other people could read! I love you, always.

"…*without Me, you could do nothing.*"

Jesus[1]

"*I can of Myself, do nothing.*"

Jesus[2]

"*For with God nothing will be impossible.*"

Jesus[3]

---

1 John 15:5   2 John 5:30s   3 Luke 1:37

INTRODUCTION

The last 10 years of my life have been crazy. Together with my wife and four children, we changed continents, left behind family and friends, and walked away from guaranteed retirement accounts. We have navigated through significant health challenges in our family and grieved with close friends who have experienced tragedy in theirs. We have been surrounded with uncertainty, from immigration to employment to income to housing. It truly has been crazy. Yet, these have also been some of the best years of our lives. I have more peace, more joy, and more satisfaction in life. My walk with God is closer and my marriage is stronger. My children are growing up with a hundred times more opportunities and they are all managing it better than me. Through it all, the one thing that has kept me sane and stable, mostly filled with hope, has been my daily connection with God through Scripture. I don't read His word in order to find some message for someone else. His word is literally my daily bread. What I hear Him speak through the pages on a daily basis is what sustains me.

I have regularly used a journal to write down the significant Scripture, understanding or application that I have received. I write it down because otherwise I would forget. I've also found that something happens when I am diligent in taking the revelatory thought and writing it down—it always gets deeper . . . and it sticks better. Periodically, I read back over what I have written and often times wonder if it was really me who wrote that!

More recently, I have found that what I have been hearing has significantly encouraged others also. Hence, during a discussion with my wife, we had a lightbulb moment. What if I trawled back through my journals and harvested a number of them to convert into a format that would help others in their own journey?

So we did. My wife, Janine, started with my raw journal entries (yes, that was a challenging experience) and fashioned them into something that would translate into other people's lives. We chose journal entries from some of our crazy times and matched the authentic stories and real-life Scriptures that have meant the world to me. They're not just words on a page. They are living words that have become life and hope in my daily life. They have been what has sustained me over the last decade. And I'm not stopping!

The way to make the most out of the following pages is to set aside ten minutes a day and just read one chapter at a time. They are structured with a story, a Scripture, an observation, and a prayer. Each chapter finishes with questions to go deeper and an action step that will challenge you to do something with what you heard that day. This is designed for you not to simply feel good as you observe our own story, but for you to personally experience and hear from God in your own life. Literally, every single day you can have a Word that comes alive to you with a specific application that you can apply on a daily basis.

My prayer is that the words on the following pages catalyze you in such a way that your personal walk with God becomes a life force of hope regardless of your circumstance. In turn, I pray that your own story becomes a catalyst of hope to those around you. May history record you as a friend of God.

Until next time, Peace to your house.

ANDY MASON
Redding, California

ONE WORD CHANGES EVERYTHING

The Word of God has the power to change us. We used to live in Hawkes Bay, New Zealand. We were happily living our lives there, surrounded by friends and family. We were a part of a great church, I had a good job, and the grandparents of our four small children lived nearby. We had it made. It had never crossed our minds that we would leave the location or the community we served. We were sensing something was about to change but couldn't figure it out. Then while on a mission trip, a friend of mine suggested that I needed to ask God whether the change was beyond where we had been looking; what if our future was in a different geographic location? When I returned home, I shared the idea with my wife, and we wrote the question down in my journal, "Is our future in this location?"

Several days later, I was reading a children's picture Bible story to my son, who was four at the time. I let him choose the story. His favorites were David and Goliath, Daniel in the lion's den, and Samson... but this evening, he chose the story of Abraham (see Genesis 12:1-3). As I read him the story, I was surprised that God spoke to me through a children's Bible! It was unexpected, but as I read, "Get out of your country... to the land I will show you..." it felt like mini fireworks going off in my heart.

Later that same week, I was listening to a visiting speaker. The message was about stepping over the line of limitations and stepping into a new land of risk and promise (see Joshua 1:2). I just sat there with a dumbfounded look on my face. And the mini fireworks I had earlier experienced were now mini-explosions. I'm sure the people around must have heard my heart thundering in my chest. I wrote down both these scriptures and pondered what they meant for us.

A couple days later, my wife, Janine, asked God to speak to her directly. If we were to make a big decision, we needed to hear together and be 100% on the same page. As she threw up the question, she immediately had a scripture reference drop into her head. "Jeremiah 3:14." She had no idea what this said, so she walked over to a chair, sat down with her Bible, and hunted for the location of the scripture. As she read, "I will take you one from a city and two from a nation, and I will lead you to Zion..." She began to weep, knowing this was going to change everything. In one week, we had gone from happily living our lives in New Zealand to knowing we were being led to leave our families, our friends, and our nation. A few very short months later, we embarked on our adventure to Redding, California.

> *And He said to them, "To you it has been given to know the mystery of the Kingdom of God; but to those who are outside, all things come in parables." It is like a mustard seed which, when it is sown on the ground, is smaller than all the seeds on earth; but when it is sown, it grows up and become greater than all herbs, shoots out large branches, so that the birds of the air may nest under its shade." And with many such parables He spoke the word to them as they were able to hear it. But without a parable He did not speak to them. And when they were alone, He explained all things to the disciples.*
> *Mark 4:11, 31-34*

God spoke His word to us. It was like a seed. It changed everything in a moment but took years to fully form. The scriptures, Bible stories, and preaching may not have spoken anything to you. But for us, it was clear that God had a plan for us in a different geographic location. That small seed has since turned into a strong tree. Many times we have felt like life was too difficult in California, that there seemed to be no way forward. Yet we had planted that original seed, the word from God, deep in our hearts, and it was growing whether we liked it or not. As we have continued to hold on to and nurture the seed, it has grown to such an extent that it (we) cannot be shaken.

Likewise, there are other seeds of the living Word of God that we have taken into our hearts and watered and nurtured. They have produced fruit because we have taken care of them. Our lives have been changed because the Word of God has come alive in us and to us. It has become something we can rely on, and in turn, it changes us. It changes everything.

The Word can seem so tiny at first as you plant it in your heart. It may seem like it has little effect on your life or the lives of those around you. But once it is planted, it can literally grow to influence nations. We are living evidence of this.

The Voice of God through His Word is louder than all the other voices around, if you will let it be so. It can be louder than the voice of the media or philosophies of man. It can be louder than the voice of world leaders or current teaching, louder than the internal voices of fear and doubt. But in order to be louder in your life, it must be grown inside of you. It must be prioritized and given its rightful place.

The Word often comes as a whisper that must be received and nurtured before it can grow. He has given us the ability to receive and understand His word. And there is a limitless supply of how much He wants to speak to you through His word. The question is, will you receive, protect, and nurture what He speaks to you?

PRAYER

Lord, thank You that Your word is alive. Thank You that it contains within it the power change everything Lord, give me eyes to see and ears to hear the Word that You will speak to me. Let me hear, receive, and nurture every word that You have already spoken. Speak to me now, Lord, that it might bring courage and hope in this very moment. Speak, Lord, for I am listening...

GOING DEEPER

- Meditate on the fact that He has said: "It was given to you to know the mysteries of the Kingdom." You have been given access to His mysteries, if you will take the time to hear them.
- What seeds has God spoken into your life? How have you nurtured those truths, in order to bring change to your life? How can you nurture those truths now?
- How can you prioritize the Word of God in your everyday schedule?

TODAY'S ACTION

What word has God spoken to you that you need to protect and cultivate today? How will you do that?

Two

SHOW ME
WHAT YOU HEARD

Have you ever wondered how it is that two people can hear the same message, but they experience it in two totally different ways? Sometimes that's a good thing. Each of us needs to hear something different on any given day. Sometimes it's a measure of how differently we are responding to what we have already heard.

The measure to which we are applying what He has already spoken will affect our future hearing. In the Kingdom, hearing is synonymous with action. What He speaks to us is not meant to be something to add to our knowledge, rather it is supposed to bring change to our lives.

Our children went to a Christian elementary school when they were young. As part of their schooling, they memorized verses about Godly attributes such as kindness, patience, and self-control. They not only needed to memorize the scriptures, but they also had declarations such as, "I am patient" or "I am kind" to learn. As the weekly test approached, they would practice the memory verses and declarations on the way to school. One day, they were making their declarations while being unkind and impatient with each other. My wife pointed out the large gap between what they were saying and what they were doing.

"It's okay," they said, "We don't actually have to do this stuff, we just have to be able to say it." Somehow, they had missed the point! The scriptures are to change us into His image. And the more we embrace the need to change and listen to what He has to say, the more we will hear in the future.

> *"If anyone has ears to hear, let him hear."*
> *Then He said to them, "Take heed what you hear.*
> *With the same measure you use, it will be measured to you;*
> *and to you who hear, more will be given.*
> *For whoever has, to him more will be given; but whoever*
> *does not have, even what he has will be taken away from him."*
> Mark 4:23-25

When we take what we have heard and value it by doing something with it, God gives us more. Think of it like this: You have two children who have been asking you over and over again for a bike. You decide it is time and give each the same gift of a shiny new bike. As they get the bike, each is grateful, thanks you politely, and shows the bike off to the rest of the family. As time goes on, though, you notice that one of your children has taken their bike and left it in the front yard. It is in danger of getting stolen and the rain is making it rusty and the paint is fading. The other child is making the most of their bike. They ride it around the neighborhood, and when it's not in use, they lock it away in the garage. This one is showing you the true measure of their gratitude.

There is a difference in how you will respond to those two children when they next ask for a gift. You love both equally, but one has, in a sense, earned your trust and qualified themselves to receive more. The other is probably going to need to do something to regain your trust before you pay for another gift.

Spiritual deafness comes because we have not been doing anything with what we have been given. Jesus said, "Take heed." Effectively, He is saying, "Listen up, be careful, pay attention." He is pointing out a spiritual law of sowing and reaping. If you sow "hearing and doing something with what you are hearing," then you will reap "more hearing."

Many times, when we are in a season that His voice seems particularly quiet, we need to look back and ask ourselves what we last heard. Did you truly respond to what you heard? Did you continue to do something with what you heard? Or did you walk away saying, "That was a great message," but went on with life as normal?

My wife has been hearing that she needs to sharpen up with her language as she drives the car. It's not that her language is terrible or that she is out of control, but she has been aware of the Lord speaking to her about "upping her game" with regard to how she reacts to the crazy drivers around our town. Having wrestled with what to do to hold herself accountable, she finally told our thirteen-year-old, "If you hear me being disrespectful about another driver, I want you to tell me, and I'll pay you fifty cents each time you do." She has actively taken steps to help her respond to what God is saying to her. So far, amazingly, she has not had to pay out any money. The very act of speaking it out and making herself accountable has helped her turn what she heard into change. Her life is showing God that she heard Him.

PRAYER

Father, thank You that you speak to me and that Your words produce life. Lord, help me to not only hear your Word but also to respond to Your Word. Let the power of Your Word bring real lasting change to my life. Open my ears to hear and open my heart to respond. I invite You to speak again to me today. I repent for the times that I have heard You speak but not responded. I ask You to forgive me and give me a fresh start.

GOING DEEPER

- What evidence is there in your life of valuing what the Lord has said to you?
- What do you do with what He says?
- How can you more effectively respond to His Word?
- Is God silent? What was the last thing you heard Him say?

TODAY'S ACTION

What is something God is speaking to you about that you need to put into practice? What will you do today to SHOW Him what you heard?

Three

PREPARE FOR INCREASE NOW

We have somewhat become experts at waiting for a breakthrough. While we still don't love the wait, we have learned how to "wait in faith," instead of becoming passive in the process. Many times, as we have waited for financial breakthrough, we have had impromptu "parties" with our kids. We buy some delicious food from the grocery store, and we tell them, "Get excited kids, our breakthrough is on its way." Did we have any actual evidence that a breakthrough was coming? No. Not at that moment. But we made it our focus to celebrate as though it was, because of what He had spoken. It has become normal for us as a family to celebrate our way into victory.

Another time we had a significant number of prophetic words about a house increase. This had gone on for years. Finally, I had another word from a stranger while traveling that said, "I feel like the Lord is saying, 'Pack your bags, I'm giving you a house.'" I immediately called home and told Janine. She, in turn, went out and purchased moving boxes and told the kids to put into the boxes anything they wouldn't be using in the next three months. We knew enough to know God's timing isn't always the same as ours, but there is always something we can do to prepare and get ready for his word to come to pass. That's what faith does.

Enlarge the place of your tent,
And let them stretch out the curtains of your dwellings;
Do not spare;
Lengthen your cords,
And strengthen your stakes.
For you shall expand to the right and to the left,
And your descendants will inherit the nations,
And make the desolate cities inhabited.
Isaiah 54:2-3

In the above passage, the author is speaking to those who are barren, to those who have lost all hope of ever having children. He is speaking to those who feel "less than" because they have been unable to produce what others take for granted. He is speaking to those who have labeled themselves as "unproductive" or a failure. He speaks to the ones who have longed for breakthrough and yearned to see a change of season. Once they expected it every month, but now, they are beyond even looking for it. For them, as for us, there is no longer expectation or excitement that a breakthrough is imminent.

We all have areas of barrenness where we no longer have hope for a breakthrough. We have, in effect, labeled ourselves as unable to produce in that area, so we don't look for breakthrough anymore. It is in those very areas that the Lord comes to us and speaks: "Hey you… yeah, you! Get ready for increase. Build a nursery. Prepare your life for change. The increase you stopped even dreaming of is now on its way. Celebrate and sing! Don't hold back at all because what you dreamed of is now coming."

I love how He speaks to every part of us. He tells us, "Go get the physical things that you need in order to manage the increase." He speaks to the emotions and says, "Let go of disappointment and the fear of being disappointed again. Embrace, through rejoicing, the change of season;

the arrival of your breakthrough is almost here. Sing, dance, get excited like you believe it is happening."

In the midst of your lack, prepare for a breakthrough. Before the increase comes, rejoice like it is already on its way. Don't wait for the first sign of pregnancy, start building the nursery now. Rejoice and celebrate His goodness. Let go of the "how" it has to happen. Let go of the "when" and simply trust that He is good and is able to do more than you ask or imagine.

PRAYER

Lord, I thank You that even in the areas I look barren, You speak increase. I choose to let go of my negative expectations for no change happening. I embrace the opportunity to celebrate before the breakthrough, knowing that You are good. I commit to doing what I need to do in order to prepare for the increase that You are bringing me into.

GOING DEEPER

- Where has God told you HE is going to bring increase?
- What can you do to prepare for the increase that He has promised is coming?
- How could you plan a pre-breakthrough celebration before the increase comes?

TODAY'S ACTION

What one practical thing could you do today to prepare for the increase—the dream you have been dreaming of?

Physically?   Financially?
Mentally?   Spiritually?
Emotionally?

Four

DO I MAKE A PLAN OR SIMPLY TRUST GOD?

Before we came to live in California, I had a plan for my future. At least I thought I did. I had studied at university and then began a job with an agricultural consultancy company. I grew in competency at my job and was growing in my spiritual walk. I had plans for what my life was going to look like. When I started dating Janine, I asked her a million questions about where she wanted to be and what she was going to be doing in ten years' time. She never had answers to my questions, but I thought I knew the answers, at least the broad details. We got married, and we moved forward together. I had a budget on a spreadsheet, an intentional plan for growth, and I knew what we were doing.

But God. In 2008, He ambushed all my plans and brought us to America.

We started from scratch again. We knew no one, we were no one, and we used up all our savings in three quick years. None of it made any natural sense. This didn't seem like good planning on God's part, and with such a big, unforeseen shift in direction, it made me wonder if it was even worth planning. Had I been doing it all wrong, having a plan? Was I just supposed to float along trusting God all this time?

A man's heart plans his way,
But the Lord directs his steps.
Proverbs 16:9

A man's steps are of the Lord;
How then can a man understand his own way?
Proverbs 20:24

The steps of a good man are ordered by the Lord,
And He delights in his way.
Psalms 37:23

I now believe that we are both supposed to plan AND to trust God with where we are going. It's not one or the other, it's both. We make our plans in connection with God, but He determines and makes strong our steps. Even on my best day, I cannot control my future.

So why should I even bother planning if God can just come in and "wreck" my plan anyway?

Proverbs 29:18 says, "Where there is no revelation the people cast off restraint." Another version (KJV) says, "Where there is no vision (plan) the people perish." So, having a plan or a clear vision helps us stay on track with our lives. Habakkuk 2:2 says to "write the vision and make it plain so those who read it may run with it." Having a written plan means that you know where you are going. At any moment, God has the right to interrupt your plan and change your direction, but at least you are not just running all over the show looking for something to do. You know where you are going, you know why you are heading that way, at least until further notice.

When you have a plan, you are also more disciplined. Because we had a plan from when we were first married, we were able to take steps to own our home, debt-free by the time God told us to move to America. That released to us the finances to live for three years with zero income. If we had not had a plan, we would have spent our money on other things and never been in the financial position to do what was required. Our plan gave us discipline in our spending.

God lets us in on His plans a little at a time. Sometimes I think that's because if He showed us all of what He planned, we would run screaming from the room in fear. We can handle just the next installment of His plan for our lives, with the grace that is currently available to us. Before we came to America, Janine had her hands full at home, raising our four small children under the age of six. It was a huge help to have her parents (aka babysitters) living in the same city as we were and my parents only a couple of hours away. Janine wasn't ready to leave that all behind to go on a crazy adventure around the world. So, when God spoke to us to leave everything, He didn't tell us it was forever. Janine identifies that as the kindness of God to her. It was easier for her to leave her family when she thought it was for nine months. Once we had lived here for that time, she was ready to hear the next step.

So, make your plans with Jesus, trusting Him along the way. Hold them lightly and be ready to respond when He changes the plans on the go. His plans were a huge upgrade on ours. It has not been easy, but it has been a wild ride and we don't regret for a moment trading in our plans for His.

PRAYER

Jesus, thank You that You have a plan for my life that is an upgrade on my own plans. Thank You that I can trust my future to You and that You will lead me and guide me. Give me ears to hear the plans that You have for me in this season. Help me to partner well with You in all that I know You have for me in this season. Give me a vision so that I may have discipline in my finances, time, and relationships.

GOING DEEPER

- What are you hearing God say about getting a vision and plan for your life?
- Where do you need to let go control of your plan and trust His plan for your future?
- Where do you lack discipline that is potentially sabotaging your future? Talk to God about His vision for that area of your life. Now make a plan to move you towards God's vision for you.
- What is God's plan for you in your current season of life?

TODAY'S ACTION

Who can you share what you just learned with and ask them to hold you accountable to trust God AND have a plan?

Five

THE IMPORTANCE OF DELAY

We live in a world of "instant." You can have coffee in an instant, meals in an instant, and information in an instant. Many things that in the past took time to build, purchase or grow can now be purchased fully developed. We have become accustomed to things being done quickly, and we are no longer required to wait for virtually anything. We become impatient if we have to wait in line for more than a few minutes in a grocery store or at the coffee shop. Our whole world has taken to inventing ways to circumvent things that take time to develop naturally.

But there is beauty in delay.

Within months of arriving to America, God began to talk to our family about giving us a house—literally "land in this land." In a natural sense, this was laughable. We had no income of any sort for the first three years and the money that we brought from New Zealand was fast being used to support our growing family. But we had great faith and took God at His Word. We connected with a real estate agent and began looking at houses in the area. It is hard to set a budget when you don't know how God was going to provide, but we looked at all sorts of houses and made a plan for what we would do when God sent the resources. We spent hours talking about what sort of income we would need to support ourselves and we wondered out loud why God was taking so long to bring the promised income and house finance. During that time, I had an advisory team that offered to help me get a business visa and quick income, but it was through a different source than the one that the Lord had talked about. I seriously thought about it for a few minutes before looking at my wife, who simply asked me, "What does Jesus say?" I sadly but clearly knew we had to turn down the offer.

The "delay" continued for FIVE YEARS. Five years may not seem long to you, but it is forever when you are longing for God to do what you thought He was going to do quickly. Those years were some of the hardest years of our lives. Yet, we can also look back and see that they were some of the most glorious years, years full of growth and expansion. They were years when we learned to trust God to a much higher degree than we had ever had to trust Him before.

> *An inheritance gained hastily at the beginning*
> *Will not be blessed at the end.*
> *Proverbs 20:21*

Let's face it, we all like it when God comes through quickly, where there is a small gap between the promise and the fulfillment of that promise. The truth is we often grow the most and have our character exposed and developed the most in the waiting. I am not a naturally patient guy. I like to get started on things before I even finish the planning stage, but I have learned to value the waiting period because it is where I most often meet God. I know that if God had given us our house right after He promised it, I would have missed out on all the growth opportunities that I experienced along the way.

As I waited, I was confronted with all the areas that I thought I trusted God but really didn't. I got a chance to truly learn to trust Him. As I waited, I discovered a whole lot of mindsets around God's desire to bless me, and I triggered a bunch of fear associated with money:

- Have I failed to steward the resources we had in the past?
- What am I missing that I should be doing?
- Will we have money for next year?
- What if something goes really bad?
- What about retirement?
- What have I done to deserve a gift of a house? Am I crazy believing like this?
- What would people say if they knew I was believing like this?
- How could I receive a gift like a house when I have friends who don't even have money for rent?
- I must work harder for this…
- Why am I second-guessing everything God has said?

Every word of the Lord is tested,
refined, and proven to be pure.
Proverbs 30:5 (paraphrased AMP/KJV)

In the midst of the delay, I certainly had plenty of opportunities to learn to wait patiently, trusting that He knew the timing better than I did. Our hearts were tested and proven in the process, something that can never happen overnight. Sure, it's frustrating. Sure, we'd still like it to be faster. But when we set our hearts to embrace what He had for us to learn in the wait, we found ourselves refined like gold. God's word has always proven true. Eventually we did get the house and it was a sweet celebration – the delay only made the realization of the dream so much sweeter.

I have four wonderful children. They have all inherited my sweet tooth, and so they love treats. When they were younger and would come to me and say, "Dad, can we hang out together and go on a date?" it was more often than not because they wanted ice cream. I was the vehicle to get them what they wanted. I would confirm this if I said: "Nah, let's just spend time together without treats." Once I'd found out their true motive, more often than not, I wanted to treat them anyway. As a good Dad, I don't always say "yes" when they ask for treats. Sometimes I say "no" for the benefit of their teeth and health. And sometimes I say "wait" knowing that if they wait, it will have so much more value for them. Sometimes I ask them to wait because I know they are not yet ready for the thing they are asking for. God is a good Father, who gives us the gift of delay for us to get to know our own hearts. Embrace the gift, there is treasure in the delay.

PRAYER

Father, thank You that You own time and You orchestrate it perfectly. Help me to be patient in the delay. Help me discover the things You have for me to learn in this season that I could never learn any other time. Grant me the faith and patience as I wait. Give me eyes to see what You are doing in my life as I wait for the promise. Show me the things that You have for me to do in the waiting period. Thank You for loving me enough to not give me everything I ask for.

GOING DEEPER

- Where do you have a delay right now? How are you responding?
- What mindsets and behaviors are being revealed in you by the

delay?

- What gift is God wanting to give you in the midst of this delay?
- Who are you finding Him to be in the midst of the delay? (God your provider, God your comfort, God your healer?)

TODAY'S ACTION

Thank God for the delay. Intentionally look around your life and identify character growth or other changes in and around you that would not have happened if you got what you wanted in an instant. Share these with someone close to you.

Six

IT'S OKAY TO DEPEND ON GOD

My wife has suffered in the last year with pain down both her arms. She is fiercely independent and doesn't like to ask for help. She likes to be strong, but in this season, she has had to learn to ask for assistance. Simple tasks have become difficult for her and her life has become smaller as she struggles with the pain. I have watched as she has learned the lesson of coming to the family to ask for help in a new way. Our love for her has not decreased because she has been "poor and needy." Our hearts have been moved with compassion, and we have been moved to help her with the things that she could normally do on her own. It has been a violent storm for her, but as she positioned herself as "poor and needy," she found help from the Lord and from others.

> *O Lord, you are my God.*
> *I will exalt you*
> *I will praise your name*
> *For You have done wonderful things;*
> *Your counsels of old are faithfulness and truth.*
> *For You have been a strength to the poor,*
> *A strength to the needy in his distress,*

A refuge from the storm,
A shade from the heat;
For the blast of the terrible ones is as a storm against the wall.
Isaiah 25:1,4

Have you ever walked or driven through a raging storm? Visibility is greatly reduced, and it is hard to see where you are going in the gloomy light. And whether it is the sound of the wind whistling around your ears or the pelting of heavy rain on the roof of your car, you know that storms also make it difficult to hear.

In times when the storm is raging around you, and it is hard to see the way forward and hard to hear His voice, He is still with you. Our God is a God who wants to give strength to us in the midst of the storm. He wants to be your refuge, your strength, and your safe place. It is a beautiful picture of a God who doesn't always calm every storm that we walk through but who wants to be our strength even in the middle of the turmoil.

We don't like to see ourselves as poor or needy. Yet it is to those who can recognize that they have need, that He comes to give His strength. He becomes our refuge from the storm and our shade from the heat when we depend on Him, even when the winds are crazy loud and the rain is beating down on us.

God is not disgusted with your need. He is moved with compassion by your weakness and wants to step in and help. He wants to do more for us than we can comprehend.

PRAYER

Father, I recognize that there are areas where I am in a storm. I feel poor and needy, and I ask for Your strength. I place myself in dependence on You. Be my strength, my shelter, and my shade from the heat today. Thank You for meeting me and being with me in the midst of this storm.

GOING DEEPER

- What feelings of vulnerability or weakness do you have in the middle of your storm?
- What will you do to depend on Him in the midst of your storm today?
- How does He want to give you or show you His strength today?
- How has He shown Himself strong for you in the past?

TODAY'S ACTION

Who can you move towards today, express where you are challenged, and ask for help?

Seven

FINDING CHRIST IN YOUR STORM

Our daughter Hannah, when she was about 15, went through a fierce storm in the form of horrific health issues. She was in constant nerve pain and could barely leave the house. Everybody we knew prayed for her, and still, she didn't get healed. Words cannot capture how hard that season was for all of us. Yet, Hannah would say that when she was sick, was the time that her faith became real; she discovered Jesus in a new way.

I can remember a time when a ministry team was coming to visit her. They were coming to pray for her to get healed, and she was nervous that strangers were going to invade her space and that it would be awkward. She was desperate enough to say yes to them coming, but she was definitely on edge. They arrived and sat and talked with her. They then began to give her gifts that they had brought for her: art supplies, a journal, and other things that she loved. These simple gifts were healing for her. She met Jesus in the midst of her storm through people hearing from Him and being obedient. When they left her body still hurt, the storm still raged, but the team that came had heard from God and brought His Presence by their kindness. He had come to her, walking on the water, to meet her in the storm.

*Immediately Jesus made His disciples get into the boat
and go before Him to the other side,
while He sent the multitudes away.
And when He had sent the multitudes away,
He went up on the mountain by Himself to pray.
Now when evening came, He was alone there.
But the boat was now in the middle of the sea,
tossed by the waves, for the wind was contrary.
Now in the fourth watch of the night Jesus went to them,
walking on the sea.*
Matthew 14:22-25

Have you ever launched out to a new place at the word of Jesus? You believed it was going to go well because He had spoken to you, but as you got "out there," you encountered angry waves and a wind that was contrary. There you are, being tossed about in the boat, and starting to doubt whether you heard Jesus right. "If He sent me here," you think to yourself, "Why am I encountering a storm?"

Many times, when we encounter an unexpected storm, we conclude that we must be on the wrong track or that we must have drifted off course. But Jesus delights to come to us in unexpected ways and surprises us by showing up. You can never know Him as the one who calms the storm if you don't ever encounter any rough waters.

His desire is for us to discover Him as the Lord of Peace in the storm. Don't assume because you are encountering waves and circumstances that are opposing you that you have wandered off course. It may be that you are in just the right place to discover Him in a new way, showing up to bring you peace and reassure you that He is with you.

PRAYER

Jesus, thank You that You are Lord of the storm. Jesus, my boat is being rocked, and the wind is trying to blow me off course. I feel alone, and I'm not sure how I am going to make it to the other side. I feel scared that I may have missed something. Would You meet me in my storm?

Lord I ask You to calm the wind and waves, and show me again that we are going to reach the other side, together.

GOING DEEPER

- Where are you headed in life that is encountering a contrary wind?
- Have you questioned whether Jesus really sent you this way because the circumstance is not lining up with what you expected?
- What do you hear Him say today as He meets you again in the middle of your storm?

TODAY'S ACTION

If you 100% believed Jesus was with you even IN the storm, what would you do differently today?

Eight

GOD IS MY ABUNDANT SUPPLY

Several times over the last few years, we have wanted to take our family on vacation but haven't really had the resources to do so. A number of times generous people have offered us accommodation in a beautiful place, but there are six of us to get there and flying isn't cheap. Each time, when we have set our hearts to ask God to supply, He has given us the finances we needed to get there and enjoy a family vacation. He has never once given us just enough to scrape by. Our family has seen abundant provision, and we have stayed in places that there is no way we could have afforded in our own ability. He loves to supply abundantly.

I once coached a friend who was struggling to believe that God would supply for her to go after her dreams. As we talked together, she realized that because they had made mistakes in their finances previously, she didn't feel like God would trust them for more than just a maintenance level of provision. Her finances were not stopping her from living her dream; her beliefs were. God wanted to supply beyond where she was at, but she didn't believe He would, so she never asked in faith.

Most of us have had seasons where we have had just enough to get by. Maybe you are starting or expanding a business, and there is not enough cash to do what you want to do. As we position ourselves to grow, it is easy to become aware that we don't have as much as we need to do all that is in our hearts. Many of us have become accustomed to asking for "just enough" to get by. It's wonderful to see God supply just enough for our day to day, but it's even better when we walk in abundance.

> *The Lord is my best friend and shepherd.*
> *I always have more than enough.*
> *Lord, even when your path takes me through*
> *The valley of deepest darkness,*
> *Fear will never conquer me, for you already have!*
> *You remain close to me and lead me through it all the way.*
> *Your authority is my strength and my peace.*
> *The comfort of your love takes away my fear.*
> *I'll never be lonely, for you are near.*
> *You become my delicious feast*
> *Even when my enemies dare to fight.*
> *You anoint me with the fragrance of your Holy Spirit;*
> *You give me all I can drink of you until my heart overflows.*
> *Psalms 23:1, 4-5*

God doesn't do maintenance. He doesn't string us along with just enough to survive. He is extravagant, expressive, generous, passionate, and abundantly beautiful. There will always be seasons where we are aware of our lack because we are in expansion mode. Our resources have not yet caught up with the vision that we have. But if you ask and expect only just enough to survive, then that is what you will get.

God wants to position you to be a person who is overflowing: overflowing with finances, overflowing with hope, overflowing with joy, overflowing with His very presence that brings solutions and peace to every situation. The issue is not His desire to fill you to overflowing. The issue is whether or not you believe He wants to do it, and whether you will position yourself to receive it.

He wants to supply abundantly for you. He wants to supply your natural needs, your spiritual needs, and for your soul. He loves to come and fill us to overflowing if we will take the time to pause and let Him do so.

PRAYER

Jesus, I am in need. You are my friend, and I believe You want to supply me until I overflow with joy, with peace, and with resources so I can be a resource of those things to the world around me. I ask You to fill me now to overflowing. Help me to raise my expectations of what You want to supply, so that I don't live in scarcity, but instead in abundance.

GOING DEEPER

- Where have you limited God's abundant supply by expecting "just enough"?
- What lies have you believed that stopped you from receiving from Him?
- What does He want to give you today that you can receive in abundance?

TODAY'S ACTION

Read the above Psalm out loud as a declaration over your life. Then do it a couple more times. What do you sense as you do this? What phrase is highlighted for you to hold onto throughout your day?

Nine

NOTHING CAN CONTAIN YOU

I once had a leader that tried to contain me. He would exert his positional leadership over me and ask me micro details about what I was doing and how I was doing it. I submitted to his leadership and followed the rules, but all the while I felt like I was living with a lid and not free to be myself. One day, when I least expected it, God stepped in and rescued me. He led me out from the restraints into a place with no restrictions. Actually, the amount of freedom scared me as for the first time I experienced leaders who trusted me more than I trusted myself. God truly released me to step into the freedom that I was born for.

The high priest rose up and all those who were with him, and they were filled with indignation, and laid hands on apostles and put them in the common prison. But at night an angel of the Lord opened the prison doors and brought them out, and said, "Go stand in the temple and speak to the people all the words of this life." And when they heard that, they entered the temple early in the morning and taught. But the high priest and those with him came and called the council together, With all the elders of the children of Israel, And sent to the

prison to have them brought. But when the officers came and did not find them in the prison, they returned and reported, saying, "Indeed we found the prison shut securely, and the guards standing outside before the doors; but when we opened them, we found no one inside!"
Acts 5:17-20, 23

In the passage above, the religious leaders of the day opposed the message of life that Peter was bringing. They put him in prison and bound him with chains. They did everything they could to control him. But then in the darkest hour, when it seemed the worst, an angel came and opened the prison door. The angel didn't just open the door but actually led him out, showing him the way at every step. No one witnessed the process, but he was made free from all restrictions the leaders had placed on him.

As you break new ground, as you work to bring life to those around you, you can expect opposition, even from those who look spiritual. You will encounter people who don't like the message that your life displays. They will try to contain you, to ask you to live smaller than God is calling you to. Your bigness of faith and vision scares people, and their response can be to try and contain you for their own sake.

The good news is that they can't contain the call of God on your life. Relax and rejoice for at your darkest hour the Lord delights to come and encounter you and lead you into freedom so that you can continue in your call. There is no man that can stop the flow of life from you.

Don't fear or resist the attempt to control you. The Lord is able to deliver us from every attempt to stop the flow of life from us. Even when it looks hopeless, like the chains are unbreakable, He has a way of walking us through the prison into freedom. Whether you are behind bars, feeling controlled, or whether you are celebrated, it doesn't really matter. You are able to speak and release life wherever you are. And just when it is the darkest hour, you will find an angel there ready to lead you out into freedom.

PRAYER

Lord, help me to speak words of life to all people, whether in a prison or not. Help me to not focus on the constraints or opposition of people around me, but rather on Your ability to lead me into life. Thank you for the life You give me. Help me to be filled to overflowing so that wherever I go people will experience Your life flowing through me.

GOING DEEPER

- What constraints are currently stopping you from fully expressing your life?
- What could it look like to live fully alive, in spite of the constraints?
- Ask the Lord to give you a picture of what living in total freedom could look like.
- What could you learn in this season that you couldn't learn any other time?

TODAY'S ACTION

Intentionally go throughout your day celebrating the gift of God in you, the message you carry, and even the challenges you face that are nothing compared to His destiny on your life. Consider putting a series of alarms on your phone to go off on the hour to remind you.

Ten

DON'T JUDGE ANOTHER'S SERVANT

Recently my wife received a distraught phone call from one of our daughters at public high school. Through the tears, she explained that she and some friends had been having a discussion that had turned to biblical things. The whole group of friends had turned on her, and she had felt dishonored and unheard. Her natural response was to point out the flaws in their reasoning (through her lens) and to think less of her friends. When our daughter got home, we heard more. The teenagers had taken something that Emily had felt very strongly about and made a case that her stand was ungodly. Ouch.

As Emily researched why she believed what she did, my wife encouraged her to step into her friend's shoes and look at why they had taken the stand they had. She encouraged Emily to see that while they didn't agree with her beliefs, they were standing for righteousness as they understood it. In the end, they had to agree to disagree, but Emily came to see that their stance did not make them "evil." And she came to appreciate the freedom that she experiences because of what she believes.

Receive one who is weak in the faith, but not to disputes over doubtful
things. For one believes he may eat all things, but he who is weak eats
only vegetables.
Let not him who eats despise him who does not eat,
and let not him who does not eat judge him who eats; for God has
received him.
Who are you to judge another's servant?
To his own master he stands or falls.
Indeed, he will be made to stand, for God is able to make him stand.
Romans 14:1-4

We all experience what Emily did that day. We all run into people who believe differently than us. Our family members, work colleagues, and those in the community around us all have different experiences and understandings of who God is and how His Kingdom operates. It's easy to feel offended when someone close to us suddenly exposes a belief that is offensive to us. Our first instinct is often to want to correct the person rather than hearing their heart and why they believe what they do.

Janine once told me of a friend she had at college called Sarah. Sarah had recently come to know Jesus and was forcefully pro-abortion. Janine figured that as Sarah got to know Jesus more, her stance would eventually change, so she kept quiet whenever the subject was raised. Finally, one day, Sarah revealed that at sixteen, she had carried a child to full term and then given her up for adoption. The experience was so incredibly painful for her that she had decided that abortion must be a less painful way to deal with an unwanted pregnancy. Janine believes that abortion is biblically wrong and does speak up about those beliefs, but it is not her job to judge another's beliefs or motives.

It is easy to judge a person's beliefs when they are different from yours, especially when you haven't heard their heart and why they believe that way. As soon as I feel contempt or judgment towards someone, I am on the way to cutting off a relationship with that person. My job is not to judge them or convince them of their wrong choices or beliefs; my job is to love them. I have the privilege of showing the love of the Father to them, whether or not I agree with their beliefs or their lifestyle. I don't have to change my beliefs to agree with theirs, but I am called to focus on what we do agree on rather than what we don't. Often, we find it difficult to disagree because our relationships are founded on our areas of agreement. When we discover that we are different, it forces us to a new level of love. It takes supernatural love to love those who oppose us.

PRAYER

Father, thank You that You loved me even when I was completely ignorant of You. Help me not to belittle those I don't agree with. Help me to see them as you see them and believe the best of them. Help me to trust that You are able to make them "stand" even when I think they don't have enough revelation to do so. Let me see the value in all those around me.

GOING DEEPER

- Where have you judged others for what they believe (or don't believe)?
- How have you judged or labeled whole groups of people who are different from you?
- What does God have to say about those people or groups of people?
- Why is it difficult to be with people who disagree with you or your values? How did Jesus do this?

TODAY'S ACTION

Identify someone around you that holds a different belief than you. Reach out to them today and hear their story, simply to grow in love and value for others (especially when you disagree with them).

Eleven

THE GIFT OF CORRECTION

I live as part of a community where "calling out the gold," is a big part of our value system. It is part of our culture to look at others through the eyes of the Father and value people for who they are and not hold them to what they are not. We choose to give grace to others as they are on the journey of growing with God. We value mercy over judgment and grace over rules.

This is a wonderful community to be a part of... until it's not. The challenge with a community like this is that many times people actually don't give me the candid feedback that I need to grow. I believe in overlooking the mistakes of others. I equally believe that we need to actively seek out feedback and correction, and we need to give the same to those who are genuinely looking to grow. Love speaks truth.

> *Wise instruction is like a costly gem.*
> *It turns the impossible into success.*
> *Love overlooks the mistakes of others,*
> *But dwelling in the failures of others devastates friendships.*

One word of correction breaks open a teachable heart, but a fool can be corrected a hundred times and still not know what hit him. Proverbs 17: 8-10 TPT

I paraphrase this as: "Wisdom seeks out correction and overlooks others' failures but foolishness hides behinds the mistakes of others and continues to miss the lesson."

Recently, Janine and I have observed a number of people receiving corrective feedback both in business and relationship environments about things that they are doing, which are not working. It is painful to watch as they go to great lengths to explain why what is happening is not their fault. In refusing to look at their contribution to the issue, they are missing an opportunity to grow.

So how do we keep a teachable heart? How do we open ourselves up for correction?

I believe that we will accept feedback to the degree that we value growth. If I simply value looking good, looking as though I have it all together, then I will resist feedback. If I really want to grow, I will be willing to take a hard look at where I am weak and receive corrective feedback. Remembering that the foundation of my value is as a child of God is critical to being able to receive correction well. With that in mind, I can now hear what people are saying to me as something that is meant to help rather than an attack on who I am.

We have four strong kids. Giving feedback can be hard at times as each of them, in their own way, wants to reject the feedback, particularly when the issue is an issue of the heart. It's easier to adjust their behavior than it is to adjust their beliefs and attitudes. It takes time for my kids to see that I am trying to help them as I address their bad attitude or their wrong thinking. They want to defend and justify or to blame others.

But it is a beautiful thing to behold when your teenager accepts the correction and grows and thrives because they have accepted what you have to say.

PRAYER

Lord, thank You that You paid the ultimate price for my complete freedom. Thank You that You sent the Holy Spirit to teach me all things. Thank You that You are always with me. Lord, give me the courage to embrace correction. Help me to see that it is a gift that has the potential to bring growth. Help me to not blame others or justify but rather to take responsibility for my mistakes. Help me to be secure enough in Your love, that I can look at where I need to grow.

GOING DEEPER

- Think of a time when have you recently received some feedback or correction. How did you respond?
- What hinders you from embracing correction?
- How does meditating on the Father's love change the way you approach feedback?
- Where is your environment currently trying to give you feedback?
- Who can you invite to speak loving correction into your life?

TODAY'S ACTION

Who will you reach out to today to get some candid feedback about how they are experiencing you or how you are navigating a particular situation?

YOU WILL NOT BE ASHAMED

"Today I want to quit, everything," I wrote in my journal. I was surrounded by pain and conflict on multiple fronts, and to make it worse my wife was also pressuring me. We had loaned money to a friend, and I didn't want to follow through on talking to them about the overdue payment. It was affecting our finances and my wife was frustrated with my avoidance of the difficult conversation. As she shared her feelings with me, I felt attacked and alone. The discussion left me feeling overwhelmed, vulnerable, and tired. Why do these discussions always seem to take place late at night?

I had so many prophetic words of God's promise to bring financial provision "now," but the promises weren't showing up in our bank account. We needed a serious injection of cash or we would lose the house we had a rent-to-buy agreement on, plus our $80,000 non-refundable deposit, plus the nine months of sweat and toil and survival through a wildfire that ravaged all around our property! It was crunch time. My daily reading that day was another scripture saying that God was going to provide, but I needed something more. Was God really going to do what He said He would do? I had always seen Him be faithful but this situation was desperate, and we needed Him to come through now.

A few days later, I was traveling from America to Australia for a friend's memorial service. This was part of the pain. "God, have I missed something? Have I stepped out ahead of you? I feel like I'm leading people to believe for the impossible, yet the hurt and pain leave me feeling disappointed… and embarrassed… and ashamed…. What am I missing?"

I arrived in Australia and had nothing to do but wait for the memorial service. I decided to go back through my journal and re-read what God had said. I was still confused. "God, what do you want to say?" I paused… then I heard a series of questions I have learned is the voice of God:

> "What day did you leave America?"
> "Sunday… March 31ˢᵗ," I replied.
> "What day did you arrive in Australia?"
> "Tuesday, April 2ⁿᵈ," I replied, adding (as if I needed to explain myself to God), "We crossed the international dateline, so I missed a day."
> "What day did you miss?"
> "April 1ˢᵗ…" It started to sink in.
> "Yes. There was no April fool's day for you. You won't be embarrassed or ashamed. I am not leading you to leave you alone. I will fulfill all that I promised you."

I just wept. Relief. Comfort. Perspective. Revelation that God is with me in this and even "orchestrated" the timing to demonstrate that He doesn't make a fool of me.

So the Lord gave to Israel all the land of which He had sworn to give to their fathers, and they took possession of it and dwelt in it. The Lord gave them rest all around, according to all that He had sworn to

their fathers. And not a man of all their enemies stood against them; the Lord delivered all their enemies into their hand. Not a word failed of any good thing which the Lord had spoken to the house of Israel. All came to pass.
Joshua 21:43-45

"Enlarge the place of your tent, And let them stretch out the curtains of your dwellings; Do not spare; Lengthen your cords, And strengthen your stakes For you shall expand to the right and to the left, And your descendants will inherit the nations, And make the desolate cities inhabited. Do not fear, for you will not be ashamed; Neither be disgraced, for you will not be put to shame; For you will forget the shame of your youth, And will not remember the reproach of your widowhood anymore."
Isaiah 54:2-4

In the gap between the promise and the fulfillment of the promise, there is always the choice to give up. As you wait for the promise to be fulfilled, you get to choose what you believe and what you will do in response to that belief. We could have tucked our tails between our legs and run for cover. We could have walked away from what God had said and found our own "Plan B." Instead, we made the decision again, and again, not to give up. What God wanted from me in that season was to wait patiently and stand courageously. To trust Him.

In Isaiah 54 (see above), God basically tells a barren woman, "Hey you, get a bigger house, because I am going to give you children." There is a response required from us when we believe that He is going to do what He said. In the above passage, it was specific: Build a bigger house. Our fear is that we take the risk and step out, only to be embarrassed or ashamed when what we believed for doesn't happen. But God is not in the business of bringing us shame. He is still in the business of fulfilling His word. For us, that meant that the finances we needed for the next step in buying our promised house came through about three (scary) months later. We are still on the journey, we are still needing to stand courageously and wait patiently, but we know that He will not leave us embarrassed or ashamed. He will not let you be embarrassed or ashamed!

PRAYER

Lord, thank You that You are with me, and You know every detail of my life. Thank You that there are no April fools with You. Lord, I put my trust in You to fulfill every promise that You have made to me. Help me to wait patiently and with great courage. Thank You that You are faithful to me and will not put me to shame. Show me how I can prepare for the promise that is to come.

GOING DEEPER

- Where have you grown weary in waiting for the promise to be fulfilled?
- Have you given up hope or reduced your expectations?
- What did God promise you? Remind Him of His promise to you. "Father, you said…."
- What do you need to do to let go of the fear of being "put to shame?"
- How can you reposition yourself to get ready for that promise?

TODAY'S ACTION

What is Holy Spirit asking you to do today to prepare for the promise He gave you?

Thirteen

DON'T CHANGE THE SUBJECT

I lead Heaven in Business—a growing global movement of people experiencing God at work and influencing the cities they serve. In the decade-long bumpy process of growing from a good idea to a sustainable plan, I have faced some significant challenges—both internal and external. Thankfully, no one has beaten me or thrown me in prison! But at some vulnerable growth points, I have had people I regard highly, question what we were doing, why we were doing it, and whether we should be doing it at all. In those moments, I felt alone and started to second guess whether I had what it would take to do this. But whenever I paused and reflected on what I heard God saying, I realized I couldn't turn away from his calling. Something burns in me that I cannot let go, even on the worst days. I feel compelled by a Higher Voice. I won't change the subject.

> *O LORD, You induced me, and I was persuaded;*
> *You are stronger than I, and have prevailed.*
> *I am in derision daily; Everyone mocks me.*
> *Then I said, "I will not make mention of Him,*
> *Nor speak anymore in His name."*
> *But [His word] was in my heart like a burning fire Shut up in my*

bones; I was weary of holding [it] back, And I could not.
Jeremiah 20:7, 9

"And now I say to you, keep away from these men and let them alone;
for if this plan or this work is of men, it will come to nothing;
but if it is of God, you cannot overthrow it—
lest you even be found to fight against God."
Acts 5:38-39

The context for the second passage above is after Jesus had ascended to Heaven, and now the reappointed Apostles were disrupting the power and control of the religious leaders. They were preaching a resurrected Jesus as the promised Messiah, with a message that empowered everyday people to have a personal and powerful relationship with their Creator. This directly confronted the religious leaders who were the ones to kill Jesus and who held power over the people through their strict rules and elitist ideology. They had arrested the Apostles and wanted to kill them also. Then one of their own, a highly regarded and godly leader, gave some sound advice, "Be careful. If this is God's work, you will not stop it and may find yourself getting into a fight against God Himself."

For the Apostles, it all came down to this, "We ought to obey God rather than men" (see Acts 5:29). The religious people of the day weren't happy about what they were doing, and they were not only vocal about it but violently opposed it. The Apostles endured being ridiculed, beaten, thrown in prison, and put in chains. Life was certainly not pleasant. Not once did they waver and stop what they were doing because of the opposition. They didn't throw up their hands in despair and say, "Well, I guess God is not with us. Perhaps He doesn't want us to do this after all." Instead, after they were beaten again and released, they went straight back to doing the thing that got them in trouble in the first place. They did not change the subject.

As you grow in your leadership and influence, you will experience opposition. The more disruptive your work or message, the more opposition you will face. At times, people will speak against you, accusing you of evil, even if you are doing what is right. You must stand with your conviction of what God has spoken to you and continue to move forward with Him, regardless of the opposition of others. Seek wise counsel to ensure you are hearing clearly and acting on your decisions with humble confidence. But remain steadfast in your calling and allow God to take care of the opposition. Don't change the subject.

PRAYER

Lord, let Your Word be a fire in my bones that I cannot hold in. Show me again how You see what I am doing. Speak to me again, the significance of my life in Your big plan. Let me be more aware of what You are saying than the voices of those around me. I choose to obey Your voice and follow my conviction rather than fear what others would say or do. I put my trust in You. Help me be strong.

GOING DEEPER

- What are you called to build? What is the message your work is communicating to those around you?
- How has opposition you may be facing attempted to reduce the volume of God's voice? What do you do when you feel surrounded by challenges?
- How will you remind yourself of what God has said for you to do, especially when the voice of opposition shouts loudly again?
- Where do you need to get back in the game, even if you have been beaten or rejected?

TODAY'S ACTION

Build an arsenal of spiritual resources you can fight with when in the middle of opposition:

- Write down life-words God has spoken to you and re-read them regularly.
- Record key go-to Scriptures as voice memos on your phone that you can play at a moment's notice.
- Seek out and build relationships with wise and mature believers who have a spirit of encouragement

Fourteen

YOU CHOOSE: MERCY OR JUDGMENT

My wife once worked with a youth pastor who was out of control. He was mean to some of the students and ruled the team of volunteers with an iron fist. He was unreasonable and no one was able to give him feedback; it was his way or no way at all. As the unhealthy pattern of behavior became more and more evident, my wife began to pray in earnest for the youth pastor. She began to cry out to God, not for judgment but for insight into what was motivating this young man. She began to feel sympathy for him and see the brokenness inside that was driving the behavior. Finally, she decided to go to the pastor who was in charge of the youth leader and let them know what was going on, but she went with a heart to help the young man rather than judgment. Her heart was turned by the decision to offer mercy instead of judgment.

There are many around you who are living lives that don't honor Christ. It is easy to see where they deserve judgment, especially where their bad decisions affect our lives. But we have a voice with God. We are His friends and as such have an opportunity to influence what happens to those around us.

And the Lord said, "shall I hide from Abraham that thing which I do; Seeing that Abraham shall surely become a great and mighty nation, and all the nations of the earth shall be blessed in him?
For I have known him, in order that he may command his children and his household after him, that they keep the way of the Lord, to do righteousness and justice, that the Lord may bring to Abraham what He has spoken to him."
Genesis 18:17-18

The above passage is just before Abraham enters into a negotiation with God over the fate of Sodom. Sodom is obviously given over to evil, and God is about to rain down judgment on them. But before God does this, He decides to talk to His friend, Abraham, and let him know what He is about to do. Abraham is a righteous man and God gives him an opportunity to be involved with the fate of a city. Abraham can stay silent, offer a proclamation of judgment or he can be the voice of mercy. Abraham chooses mercy and begins a dialogue with God to ask for mercy for the sake of the few righteous within the city.

Psalms 2:8 says that we can ask for nations as our inheritance, the ends of the earth for our possession. We have an opportunity to influence the wellbeing of people, cities, and nations by what we declare, by what we pray, by how we intercede for them. I choose to declare mercy for the nations of the earth!

Jesus amplified this statement a whole lot more by stating to his disciples that whoever they forgave would be forgiven (see John 20:23). Pause and think deeply on that one!

Jesus modeled mercy and forgiveness AND he was never shy at confronting people around him. He confronted the religious leaders, people in their sin, the crowd who followed Him, His own family, and His closest disciples. Be careful that we are not ignoring judgment (speaking truth) as we declare mercy. Truth is the only pathway to real freedom. We are able to speak truth in love because we have internally already partnered with mercy.

PRAYER

Father, thank You that You forgave me before I even knew I needed it. Thank You for showing me how to walk through betrayal and injustice. I choose to declare mercy over the people around me whose bad decisions affect my life. Grant them mercy, that they will have the opportunity to humble themselves before they find themselves at Your seat of judgment. Grant me the wisdom and courage to speak truth with love and hold people to account.

I declare mercy over my city and my nation. I choose forgiveness. Let Your mercy triumph over judgment, and Your kindness lead to a change of heart.

GOING DEEPER

- Who have you judged because of their "crazy" actions?
- Pray and ask the Lord to show you what drives them to those actions.
- Actively speak mercy over those people. Pray for their wellbeing and ask the Lord to intervene.

TODAY'S ACTION

After praying through your heart posture of mercy, who will you go and speak truth or give feedback to today?

Fifteen

CHOOSE TO WORK WITH GOD'S HAND

God had been promising us a house of our own in America for quite some time, and we had done everything we knew to do to partner with God to make that happen. As a family, we had done prophetic acts (many times over), and we had celebrated the victory before we saw any sign of it coming to pass. We had talked numerous times about what we could possibly do to bring in more money in order to save for a deposit for the promised house. But each time we were tempted to take matters into our own hands, we stopped and asked the Lord what He wanted us to do. Each time the answer was the same. "Nothing. Just wait and trust Me."

Now when the people saw that Moses delayed coming down from the mountain, the people gathered together to Aaron, and said to him, "Come, make us gods that shall go before us;
for as for this Moses, the man who brought us up out of the land of Egypt, we do not know what has become of him."
Exodus 32:1

"And they made a calf in those days, offered sacrifices to the idol, and rejoiced in the works of their own hands."
Acts 7:41

The Israelites were like us, they were waiting for a promised breakthrough. And it seemed like Moses and God were both in a holding pattern and not in any hurry to fulfill the promise the people had been waiting for. The Israelites waited for Moses to come back down the mountain, but when he didn't, they decided to take matters into their own hands. They made an idol that they could worship as "god." The Israelites had seen God literally go before them as a pillar of cloud by day and a pillar of fire by night, but now they were asking Aaron to make them a "god" that could go before them. Remember also, that this is after they had seen the God of breakthrough work on their behalf in parting the Red Sea and providing manna from Heaven on a daily basis. They had seen His goodness up close and personal, but in the pressure of waiting, in the desire to control the timetable of God, they decided to just "do something."

Sometimes we do need to do something. We are in a partnership with God, and He is waiting for us to take the next step. But many times, we are driven to do something because we want to be in control and doing nothing but waiting for God exposes our fear and insecurity and lack of trust. We are people of action. We are business people who know how to get our ducks in a row and make things happen. When things are not happening on the timetable that we think they should, it is frustrating and uncomfortable. There are tension and uncertainty and a feeling of being out of control in simply waiting for God to come through and do what He said He would do.

When we are in those situations, our natural inclination is to take charge and to relieve the tension by making progress even if the progress is not really in the right direction. We want to build something so people can see what we are doing. Instead, focus on the work that God is doing and stick to that. At the end of your life, it will be more important that you can say, "Look what I built with the Lord," than "Look what I built with my own hands." Sometimes the thing that He is asking us to do seems counterintuitive to the solution we are looking for. When we were waiting for a financial breakthrough, it seemed logical for us to look for a second job. Yet instead, we felt God say to simply trust Him and continue to invest in building His Kingdom as we were already doing. To fully invest in doing His work, we had to let go of our desire to control the outcome and the timetable.

PRAYER

Father, I am tired of waiting for Your promise. I recognize I want certainty more than I want You. Thank you for showing me that. I let go of control. Please forgive me and keep my heart on what is most important. I don't want to build anything without You being part of it. Help me grow in patience and trust.

GOING DEEPER

- Where is your desire for control driving you to "just make something happen?"
- Where is the tension of uncertainty influencing you to let go of simply trusting God?
- Spend some time remembering how He has led you to this point in your life. What does this say about how He will continue to lead you?

TODAY'S ACTION

Before launching into all your tasks for today, pause and ask the Holy Spirit what tasks He would have you focus on. Write those down. Does His list surprise you? Next, what strategy does He have for you to advance? Be still and quiet your thoughts for a moment. Then write down the first thoughts that come to mind.

Sixteen

KEEP WALKING. YOU CAN DO THIS!

The Lord had promised us a house of our own in the USA. He had promised us "land in this land," and He had promised us financial breakthrough over and over again. We had received prophetic word after prophetic word and testimony after testimony confirming this direction. He had spoken through Scripture time after time, and we believed Him. But after years of waiting, the journey was wearing us thin and hope was dwindling. We were broadsided by vehicle costs and children's dental costs and wondered at what point should we cut our losses and return to New Zealand. And yet, God continued to speak about this being our "promised land" and that we would have "land in this land."

We had a choice to make. We could either get cynical or we could renew our expectation of His goodness showing up and start to celebrate, to choose joy over discouragement. It cost us letting go of our discouragement and the desire to control our circumstances. But when we did, we began to experience more joy and see His provision even before the breakthrough fully came.

But immediately Jesus spoke to them, saying,
"Be of good cheer! It is I; do not be afraid."
And Peter answered Him and said,
"Lord, if it is you, command me to come to You on the water."
So He said, "Come." And when Peter had come down out of the
boat, he walked on the water to go to Jesus.
But when he saw that the wind was boisterous, he was afraid;
and beginning to sink he cried out, saying, "Lord, save me!"
And immediately Jesus stretched out His hand and caught him, and
said to him, "O you of little faith, why did you doubt?"
Matthew 14:27-31

In the story above, Peter and the disciples were in another boat, in yet another storm where the conditions were against them. Jesus had sent them ahead while He closed down the previous meeting and had some alone time with His Father. Then Jesus came to them in the middle of the night. When they saw Him walking on the water towards them, they were afraid, thinking they were seeing a ghost. But Jesus said, "Be of good cheer. It is I. Do not be afraid." Peter responded boldly, and at Jesus's word got out of the boat, walking on the water. But as Peter found himself away from the protection and security of the boat, standing on something impossible and surrounded by waves and wind, he began to freak out and second-guess his decision to step out (so would I!). As he and his faith began to sink, he desperately cried out to Jesus, who immediately responded by grabbing his sinking hand and walking together with him back to the boat. Then everything became calm . . . of course!

The disciples, including Peter, had been with Jesus, watching miracle after miracle. Just before their boat ride, they had been watching and participating in the multiplication of a handful of food to feed a multitude. They, themselves, had picked up the leftovers, which amounted to MORE than what they had started with. Yet just a few hours later, they didn't even recognize Jesus as He came to them. They were filled with doubt and fear. Peter, once he realized that it was Jesus, pushed past his doubt long enough to jump out onto the water. But he quickly succumbed to fear again and began to sink.

I've heard this passage preached different ways: Peter the impulsive and easily distracted disciple whose faith oscillated like the waves; or Peter the courageous, who responded to Jesus's voice with faith, took a risk, and did the impossible while the others simply looked on. The heart of the matter is, the disciples, including Peter, are just like us. They experienced the miraculous provision and goodness of God, only to forget all in a moment when the next challenge came. Like us, Peter had a "flash" of motivating faith, as he recognized Jesus in the situation. But like us, he also took his eyes off the goodness of God and put his eyes on the size of the storm.

In the midst of it all, Jesus simply says, "You chose doubt, but you could choose faith. You chose fear, but you could choose joy" (my paraphrase Matthew 14:31). Nehemiah 8:10 says, "Do not sorrow, for the joy of the Lord is your strength." Where does the joy come from, especially in the midst of the storm? It comes from knowing that even when the storms are big, Jesus is bigger than the storm, and He is coming to us. Our confidence is not in our ability to hold onto Him but in His ability to hold onto us. Our confidence comes from trusting His ability. When we choose to focus on that reality, we can choose joy in the storm and step out to meet Him in the uncertainty, knowing that He will hold us up.

PRAYER

Lord, thank You that You are the God of all creation. You own the weather. You are bigger than the storm. You can walk on water. Lord help me to choose joy over fear and faith over doubt, even as

I walk through my own circumstance of adversity and uncertainty. Thank You that You are always good towards me, and You will not let me drown.

I refuse to be impressed by the size of the storm; I choose to focus on how great You are and that You are with me. Period! I let go of control. I trust You. I choose joy!

GOING DEEPER

- Where have you seen God's goodness 'show up' in your life that gives you something to hold onto until His goodness shows up again?
- Where is Jesus asking you to step out onto the water, because you know it is His voice speaking to you?
- What would you do differently in your storm if you were fully convinced that He is coming to meet you?

TODAY'S ACTION

Consider how it may have been different for Peter if the eleven disciples still in the boat had started cheering him on when he started to waver. "Come on, Peter! You've got this! Keep going!"

Who do you know that is currently in a situation of risk and uncertainty, having stepped out of their "boat"? Do something today to reach out and encourage them as they "walk on water."

Seventeen

YOU HAVE MORE INFLUENCE THAN YOU REALIZE

I once met a person who was a teacher aide in an elementary school and was struggling with what was happening in the classroom. She asked God for wisdom and got an idea that became a solution to a problem she and those around her were facing. She gained permission from the teacher in charge to implement the idea and soon found herself before the district superintendent, who wanted her to share and implement the strategy over the whole of the school district. She went from the lowest rung on the teaching ladder with no apparent influence over policy, to teaching all the teachers in the district the concept that God had given her. What influence!

We don't always have the positional authority to significantly influence a given situation or organization. It is true that the person with the leadership role can bring change more easily than one who is "just an underling," but God can interrupt the normal flow of things to bring change to any environment when He has a son or daughter in the picture. When you are walking in His ways, you influence your surroundings far more than you realize. What if we did this intentionally?

Now when neither sun nor stars appeared for many days, and no small tempest beat upon us, all hope that we would be saved was finally given up. "And now I urge you to take heart, for there will be no loss of life among you, but only of the ship. For there stood by me this night an angel of the God to whom I belong and whom I serve, saying 'Do not be afraid, Paul; you must be brought before Caesar; and indeed God has granted you all those who sail with you.' Therefore take heart, men, for I believe God that it will be just as it was told me.
Acts 27:20, 22-25

The Apostle Paul, now a prisoner, was being transported under guard to Italy, where he would be brought to trial before Caesar. As a prisoner, he had no say in what was to happen along the way. Yet he advised his guard that they should not sail beyond a certain location because of the weather and his intuition that the trip would end in disaster and much loss. Unsurprisingly, Paul's advice was ignored, and they set sail. A few days later, as Paul predicted, the weather went crazy and the ship and passengers were in a perilous position. After many days like this, all on board gave up hope of surviving the situation. Then Paul was visited by an angel who told him all would be well for him and those on board. The lowly prisoner brought hope and direction to his guard, to the ship's captain, the sailors, and the other passengers. In a natural sense, he had the least influence. But in the midst of the crazy situation, he was the one who brought hope, direction, and deliverance to ALL those on board.

We are each on some sort of "ship." This may be a work or team role or business we lead. We may not be prisoners as Paul was, even if some days it feels like that! However, there are many times we can feel powerless regarding where the organization is headed or how it is going to get there. Sometimes the crazy times are because of other people's decisions. We need to speak up when we can, but even if we are ignored, simply our presence in that environment and remaining connected to the God will have more influence on the outcome than we could ever have imagined. Notice that all the other prisoners, guards, sailors, and passengers got to live simply because Paul was with them—276 people in total (see Acts 27:27). Paul brought life to them just by virtue of being in their midst and staying aware of what God wanted to do. God met them in the middle of the storm. All of them. Regardless of social status, positional status or religious status. God didn't rescue Paul out of the storm and leave the others there to die. In this instance, God didn't calm the storm, He let the storm rage but placed Paul there to bring a solution that delivered the entire group.

At one point, some of the sailors tried to sneak off the ship leaving the others behind. Paul grabbed his guard, "Hey, don't let them leave! They must stay on board for us all to be saved." To this, the soldiers immediately cut away the lifeboats so no one could escape. The entire group on board was saved because Paul chose, even from his lowly position as a prisoner, to speak up. He let them know what God was saying and then let them choose whether or not they would respond. Likewise, there will be situations where you may not have the seemingly necessary position to speak up in a given situation, but you can still have influence if you are prepared to let your voice be heard. They initially rejected Paul's advice not to sail, but he didn't get offended and stay silent in the future. He stayed humble, and when he had the opportunity again, he spoke up and as a result, saw every single person with him delivered from certain death.

It's interesting to note that in this obvious deliverance from death by the hand of God, that nothing was mentioned about the spiritual salvation of the people on board. It was purely a deliverance from physical death. It wasn't so that Paul could preach Jesus to the passengers; it was so that Paul could get where God wanted Him to get, and those around him on the way got to benefit. Wow. When we are present with God, we have more influence on our surroundings than we realize!

PRAYER

Father, thank You that You are with me. Thank You that You lead and guide me in all situations. Thank You that you have solutions to every situation regardless of how I feel. Show me those You have given into my care . . . my influence. Let me feel towards them how You feel towards them. I forgive those who have ignored my voice and the wisdom You have given me. Give me the courage to speak up and wisdom to know what to say. Help me to stay aware of how You see every situation I face. Thank You for delivering me and those around me from all harm.

GOING DEEPER

- What situation are you facing right now where you have allowed your influence to be less than what God is saying? What will you do about this?
- Who do you need to forgive for rejecting your advice or reducing your voice (consider forgiving yourself also)?
- Whose life is dependent on you speaking up?
- Ask God who he has placed in your care. Start praying for their wellbeing.

TODAY'S ACTION

Intentionally partner with God for all those with or around you—at home, at work. Take some time to walk around your house and pray for all those you live with. Head to work early or stay a little later and intentionally walk around the entire building, praying for the wellbeing of all those within your influence. Journal what happens over the next few weeks.

Eighteen

MAKE THE DECISION!

As a young adult, I was full of fear that I would miss out on God's perfect plan for my life. I would pray and ask Him for guidance but always had nagging doubts that undermined my confidence in making decisions. "What if I get it wrong?" "What if I decide and then miss out on the best God has?" "How do I know which decision is the RIGHT decision?" The underlying fear of failure resulted in double-mindedness and procrastination when it came to decision making and this was not fun.

Around that time, I fell in love with my best friend and wanted to ask her to become my wife. I asked God what He thought and heard nothing. Finally, I sensed He was saying that He trusted me to choose and that He would bless MY decision. Now I had no excuse. I planned the proposal—a mountaintop sunrise event, complete with a song I had written for the occasion. All went smoothly and she said "Yes!" We were excited to begin this new season together.

We had been engaged for a few months and had started preparations for the wedding when my fear started to show up. I began to second-guess my decision. "Are you sure this is right? If you get this decision wrong, it will mess up the rest of your life . . . (not to mention hers!!!)" My fiancé started to sense what was silently going on in my head. During one late-night discussion, she asked me what was going on. I fumbled about trying to answer but nothing came out very well. What became evident to her was that I was afraid that marrying her was not the right decision. The evening ended with her taking off her engagement ring, putting it into my hand, and with tears in her eyes saying, "I thought when you gave me this ring, you were certain you wanted to marry me. If you are not sure, then I want you to have the ring back. When, and if you are sure you want to marry me, you can give me the ring again." The indecisiveness from the fear of failure had not just hurt me; now, my wavering decision was hurting the person closest to me.

I was following God with all my heart, but fear had found a way to undermine my ability to trust His leading. In theory, I believed that God could direct me as long as I kept my heart towards him. But I needed more. Could I really . . . really trust God with my future?

> *As he [Saul] journeyed, he came near Damascus,*
> *and suddenly a light shone around him from heaven.*
> *Then he fell to the ground, and heard a voice saying to him,*
> *"Saul, Saul, why are you persecuting Me?"*
> *And he said, "Who are You, Lord?" Then the Lord said,*
> *"I am Jesus, whom you are persecuting.*
> *It is hard for you to kick against the goads."*
> *So he, trembling and astonished, said, "Lord, what do You want me*
> *to do?" Then the Lord said to him, "Arise and go into the city, and*
> *you will be told what you must do."*
> *Acts 9:3-6*

Saul was basically a terrorist, except his actions were sanctioned by the leading religious authority in his nation. He was spending his days looking for Christians to persecute. Violence was simply part of the process. He was 100% opposed to Christians and 100% zealous for God. He was devout but deceived. This was genocide. His mission was to root out all the crazy followers of Jesus and eradicate them from the planet. And it looked like he was succeeding. In the middle of his killing spree, as he was looking for more Christians to persecute, Jesus did an intervention. Saul wasn't looking for Jesus. He thought he was doing the right thing in serving God. But God loved him enough to reach out to him despite him being "murderous." When Jesus knocked him off his transport and spoke audibly, Saul immediately responded by saying: "What do you want me to do Lord?" He instantly transformed from being against Jesus to working for Him. If God can meet Saul and interrupt him from making horrifically bad decisions, how much more can He direct our paths when our hearts are directed towards Him?

In one moment, God changed a terrorist's direction and He can do the same for us. There is no need to be in great fear over decision making when we put our lives in His hands. Notice how fast Saul responded to Jesus once He realized who He was. If we are making decisions the best we know and walking with Jesus the best we know, He is more than able to adjust our direction along the way if necessary. So trust Him and make the decision!

(By the way, deciding to marry Janine was the best decision I ever made. After 21 years, four children, two continents, and many challenges, we are still best friends and growing stronger every day.)

PRAYER

Jesus, You are my Savior and Lord. I surrender my life to Your ways. Thank You that You promise to direct my path and lead me in all truth. Thank You that Your ability to lead and adjust me is much greater than my ability to make decisions, good or bad, even if I am behaving ignorantly or being deceived. Thank You that You can send people, angels, or circumstances to get my attention to get me back on track.

Lord, keep my heart soft so that I quickly respond to your whisper. Thank You that You trust me to make decisions. I trust You.

GOING DEEPER

- Where has the fear of "getting it wrong" stopped you from moving forward?
- Where is God currently giving you the opportunity for a transformational experience?
- Meditate on the fact that God loved a terrorist enough to encounter him on the way to more terror. If God can move a terrorist, how much easier can he move you?
- Declare: "I am a powerful decision-maker, designed to co-create with God. I make great decisions!"

TODAY'S ACTION

Make a decision (especially if there is something you are procrastinating about). Let your decision be a practical expression of worship as you do, so trusting Him to lead and adjust you moving forward. Express gratitude for His leading before making the decision. Then make the decision and write down the next action step. Then express gratitude to Him again for continuing to lead you in wisdom and truth. Your decision-making ability just became an act of worship!

Nineteen

YOUR LEADER IS NOT YOUR LIMITATION

I am surrounded by people who have walked with God for decades, and they have the life lessons and body scars to prove it. We call these people spiritual fathers and mothers. I am privileged to have Danny Silk and Kris Vallotton be two of the godly leaders who have personally and significantly spoken into my life. But it hasn't always been this way. I haven't always had people like this around me and I have also experienced natural and spiritual leaders who have misunderstood me, undermined me, and tried to control me. And these are people who love God and seek to serve Him to the best of their ability. I assumed they would all see and celebrate my growth, but I have learned that people are people everywhere you go—we all have insecurities and fears. At the time, my experiences with these leaders left me feeling rejected, alone, and confused. This revealed that I believed my success was determined by them recognizing and promoting me.

But God was with me. Through those painful experiences, I learned that it is God who promotes, regardless of what people do around me. I learned that my identity and value are not based on whether or not I am recognized or promoted by my local leadership; my identity and destiny have already established by my Father in Heaven. Jesus paid the price for me to become all I am destined to be and all things are working for me toward that outcome. I learned that God is still with me, even if I am rejected or overlooked or undermined. I grew strong in my belief of God's goodness being at work despite the crazy circumstances that sometimes surrounded me. And I found that God can promote and give favor even when fathers around me don't. In the end, my favor and friendship with God and what He says about me is more important than what others say or don't say.

> *And the patriarchs, becoming envious, sold Joseph into Egypt.*
> *But God was with him and delivered him out of all his troubles*
> *and gave him favor and wisdom in the presence of Pharaoh, King of*
> *Egypt, and made him governor over Egypt and all his house.*
> *Acts 7:9*

Joseph was rejected, undermined, and sold out by his ten older brothers—the Patriarchs (co-founders of the 12 tribes of Israel). The Patriarchs were jealous of his God-given favor so they trafficked Joseph as a slave into a foreign country. But Joseph ended up second-in-charge of the entire country in which he was introduced as a slave because God had another destiny for him. That is some promotion!

If you have ever felt rejected by your natural or spiritual family—by the fathers in your life of whom you thought would be your biggest supporters, then you are in good company! Almost every leader that we see in the Bible has a story where they had to face standing alone in order to discover that God with them was all that truly mattered. It's the same today. There will always be moments when you feel like you stand alone, when no one understands and the world seems to be against you. The key in all these situations is to recognize what God is doing. There are no perfect leaders, but everyone contributes something to the process of us coming into our full destiny, if we keep our heart in the right place.

Joseph said to them [referring to his brothers who betrayed him],
"Do not be afraid, for am I in the place of God?
But as for you, you meant evil against me; but God meant it for good,
in order to bring it about as it is this day, to save many people alive.
Genesis 50: 19, 20

Joseph had multiple opportunities to get offended with God and with life: some of his brothers plotted his murder; he was sold into slavery; he was falsely accused and thrown into prison; and he was even forgotten by those he helped succeed in prison. His road to becoming a leader of the nation and part of Pharaoh's own household was not exactly the path of glory and ease. His pathway of betrayal launched him into his destiny because God was with him and he refused to partner with the offense that he could have easily justified. He understood that even though leaders may intend evil toward us, God can use it for good.

Now, this does not mean that our only pathway to promotion is at the hands of a difficult father or leader. Malachi 4:6 talks about God turning the hearts of the fathers to their children and the children to their fathers. *This is God's best design.* But whether we are celebrated and promoted by the fathers in our life, or rejected and betrayed, God has a way of promoting us to where He wants us to be. The real question is, who are we becoming in the process? Are we learning to trust in the fact that God is with us, or are we allowing the pain of what we are experiencing to turn us inward—bitter, offended, and self-absorbed? The second choice only extends the pain and delays the work of God in us.

God is with us, period. Our future is in His hands. He is not limited by our leaders or our circumstances, regardless of what it feels or looks like. Once we truly understand this, we can relax and trust Him. If He is with us in the dungeon, then the dungeon can become a place of growth and communion with Him. If He is with us in the palace—a place of promotion and success, then that also is a place of communion with Him.

PRAYER

Lord, let my heart stay soft towards my leader's even when they misunderstand, reject, or undermine me. Let the revelation that You are with me penetrate my heart so that every place I find myself becomes a place of communion with You and a springboard into greater things. I choose not to partner with offense or unforgiveness.

I forgive [*name the leaders you need to forgive*] for [*be specific how they have affected you*]. Father, thank You for Your unending Presence with me. I trust You alone with my future.

GOING DEEPER

- Where do you feel abandoned by those who you thought would protect you? Meditate on the fact that even in the midst of that, God was (and is) with you.
- What is God asking you to let go of? (offense, bitterness, hurt. . .)
- What is God giving you in return?
- What will you do to help remember that He is with you?

TODAY'S ACTION

God is in your future; stay close to Him and you will get there also! Your future is in His hands. If we keep our hearts right, every leader we have, good and bad, will shape us for good. Send a note or text to a leader (past or present) identifying the good attributes they have helped you grow in.

Twenty

ARE YOU CRAZY, OR IS THIS THE POWER OF GOD?

In 2008, we were living our lives in Hawkes Bay, New Zealand. I had a healthy family, a great job, close friends; we had just paid off all our house debt and I was a part of the leadership team for the local church we served. It looked like we were positioned to prosper financially, relationally, and spiritually. We had no intention or thought of moving. But while I was on a mission trip to Uganda and talking with a friend, he encouraged me to ask God if our future was in the location where we lived. I returned home and together with my wife prayed and asked the Lord that question: "Is our future in this location?" To our astonishment, within one week He replied emphatically, "No." That began our journey to a new nation. Six weeks after we heard from God, we landed in Redding, California, with our nine suitcases and four young children.

Originally, we thought that maybe we would be in Redding for nine months while I attended Bethel School of Supernatural Ministry. But it quickly became apparent, and God spoke clearly, that we were here for an extended period of time. With no income or support for three full years and a house full of growing kids, our finances became depleted and it looked like our decision to move nations was not a wise one.

Family and friends were supportive, but many didn't understand the decisions we were making and thought we were crazy. "Why leave New Zealand when you could have all the life success you want here?"

The Spirit of God filling us and leading us can look crazy to those observing. In Acts 2, the disciples were gathered together waiting for the Holy Spirit to be poured out. He finally came like a rushing wind and filled them up, placing what looked like a tongue of fire on each one's head. That is unusual! Then they began immediately speaking in other languages without having learned them! Wow! There were many God-fearing people from all different nations in Jerusalem at the time. These people heard the commotion and came running to see what was happening. Each one saw then heard the disciples telling the wonders of God, in their own language.

> *So they were amazed and perplexed saying to one another*
> *"Whatever could this mean?"*
> *Others mocking said, "They are filled with new wine."*
> *Acts 2:12-13*

The crowd that gathered that day didn't know what to do with what they were seeing and hearing. Some marveled and were curious enough to ask what it meant. Others simply mocked them and assumed they were drunk even though it was early in the day. In the midst of the noise and confusion, Peter stood up and began to preach. He explained that what they were seeing was the promise that the prophet Joel had spoken about—that God's Spirit would be poured out on all people. When Peter finished preaching, three thousand people responded to the invitation to follow Jesus and also be filled with the Holy Spirit.

> *Now when they heard this, they were cut to the heart,*
> *and said to Peter and the rest of the apostles,*
> *"Men and brethren, what shall we do?"*
> *Acts 2:37*

There were two groups of people in the crowd: those that mocked what they saw, and those who didn't necessarily understand, but who were open to learning more. When God shows up in power or when He speaks to people and leads them in a way we don't expect, we always get to choose how we respond. Will we respond with, "This is crazy, they must be out of their minds," or will we respond with, "God, are you in this? What are you doing?"

> *When they heard this, they were furious and plotted to kill them.*
> *Acts 5:33*

> *When they heard these things they were cut to the heart,*
> *and they gnashed at him with their teeth.*
> *Acts 7:54*

As we pursue God and see His wisdom and power evidenced around us, there will be people who think we are crazy and seek to discredit us. The power of God working in us and through us, demanding a response. For those around us, it comes down to this: "If we acknowledge that what just happened to them is God, then we must pay attention and respond to Him. But if we can discredit their character, we can convince ourselves that what happened was just circumstance and we are justified in doing nothing."

As we have walked this journey of responding to the voice of God, we know that the people watching our lives have been polarized in their response. Some have celebrated with us observing the miracles we have seen along the way. Our faith and experience with God have catalyzed them on their own journey of faith and miracles. Others, however, have drawn back from us, believing that we are crazy for living the way we live. It hurts, but we cannot be moved by people not understanding our walk with God. We cannot be moved by their mockery or discomfort with our lifestyle. Instead, we must continue on with Him, knowing that our lives can draw others into a relationship with Him.

PRAYER

Father, Your thoughts are higher than my thoughts, and Your ways higher than my ways. Help me always seek to know what You are saying to me, especially when I see Your Spirit moving but I don't understand. Help me to draw near to You and what You are doing, and never to stand with the mockers because it doesn't look like I expected it to. Help me not be deterred because others think my life is crazy, when they don't understand how You are moving in me and through me.

Help me not draw back because my life feels embarrassing or makes others uncomfortable. I give up my right to understand what You do. I trust You alone.

GOING DEEPER

- Where have you drawn back from pursuing the Lord because it looked crazy or embarrassing, or people close to you made fun of your decision?
- How could you make a decision before God, to let go control and move towards Him in this area?

- Are there people you need to forgive who have mocked or drawn back from you on your journey? Ask the Holy Spirit to show you what was really going on in their lives and release them from your expectations. Pray blessings over them.

TODAY'S ACTION

Take a moment and invite the Holy Spirit to fill you to overflowing with His goodness and power. What is one thing you can do today to fully embrace letting go control and trusting the Holy Spirit's leading?

For more on this topic, see Benny Hinn's book, *Good Morning Holy Spirit*.

Twenty One

WHOSE PRIORITY WILL YOU PROTECT?

A number of years ago, I had an unofficial advisory board help me with a ministry that I was building. The board was made up of Godly men who were successful in the area I was working in. God had connected me with each one and though they all believed in what I was doing, each had their own priorities and ideas about how the ministry should be run. One day, after a particularly difficult meeting, one of them walked out with me and candidly said, "Andy, you just wasted five hundred dollars of my time." I was cut to the heart and responded, "What could I do differently?" He answered, "Nothing. There are different agendas under the table." This truth-filled feedback made me realize that even though God had given me a clear picture of what I was to build, I was allowing the collective genius of the leaders around me pull us in a different direction. That was my last meeting with the advisory board. I gently disbanded it and then walked for a season on my own.

That meeting was one of a number of times when I have had to decide if I will be influenced by the crowd or whether I will follow my own conviction of what is needed. My friends at that time had an agenda (not necessarily a bad one) that just wasn't what I was hearing from God. I had to stand up internally and decide whether what God was saying was more important to me than what these proven and trusted men of God were saying. It was a difficult decision because all of them were more mature, more affluent, and more influential than I was. I wrestled with accusing thoughts that I was being unteachable. Over time I came to see that it was all part of my necessary growth as a leader. I needed to stand alone for a season, simply trusting myself to hear what God was saying. Years later, I have established the priority of hearing first from Heaven and not deferring to someone else who looks like they would know better than me. Now I have another group of advisors who add wisdom, strategy, and momentum to what we are building.

In Acts 9, Peter is called to the bedside of Tabitha, who has recently died. The room was full of close friends who were weeping and showing Peter the garments that Tabitha had made for them. Peter was pulled into an atmosphere full of grief and loss. No one (from the Bible's account) was praying or believing in resurrection. There was no hope in the room, only the profound sense of loss that follows the death of a beloved member of the community. Peter had to choose whether he would be influenced by the prevailing atmosphere in the room (grief and loss) or whether he would create a different atmosphere where the impossible could happen. Check out what happened:

> *But Peter put them all out and knelt down and prayed.*
> *And turning to the body he said, "Tabitha arise."*
> *And she opened her eyes and when she saw Peter she sat up.*
> *Then he gave her his hand and lifted her up;*
> *And when he had called the saints and widows, he presented her alive.*
> *Acts 9:40, 41*

Peter actually chased the grieving friends out of the room so that he could focus on what God wanted to do, without being overwhelmed by the prevailing negative atmosphere. He quieted his world, ignored the body, and began to pray. After an undisclosed time, when he had become more aware of Heaven's perspective, he turned to the dead body and simply commanded, "Tabitha arise." Suddenly, the reality of Heaven invaded earth and Tabitha was resurrected from the dead.

In order to release the reality of Heaven on the earth, you first have to become aware of it in for yourself. What is God saying in this situation? What is God doing here? Many times we are pulled into a situation in our own lives or the lives of those around us where the current reality is not the manifestation of Heaven on earth. Maybe our financial situation is crazy or a friend or family member is sick or dying. If we allow our attention to dwell on the earthly reality of the bank balance or the doctor's report, we can lose our connection with the higher reality of Heaven. I am not talking about being in denial of what is happening, rather I am talking about facing the facts with the superior reality of Heaven's perspective.

Heaven's perspective can only be consistently experienced when we make His priority more important than any other. When we become more aware of Him, we become more aware of His goodness and His bigness, and His ability to intervene on our behalf. In His Presence, we become aware that we are His children, made in His image, carrying His power and authority to change any circumstance. And in His presence, we become aware that He is with us and wants to work through us. If we are to truly be influential on the earth, if we are to bring positive change in our communities, then we must make His priority our priority. When we seek first His Kingdom and righteousness, there is no place for second.

PRAYER

Lord, help me to prioritize my connection with You, not so that I can accomplish some great mission, but FIRST for the delight of my relationship with You.

Help me to become more aware of Heaven's reality—Your love, power, and goodness, than the reality of the challenges that confront me. Give me the courage to lead from Heaven's perspective, regardless of the circumstance, and be the influencer in the room rather than the one who is influenced.

GOING DEEPER

- Where have you allowed the people or facts in front of you to distract you from an awareness of what is possible with God?
- What does God want to say about that circumstance?
- How do your daily choices and weekly schedule reflect the priority of your connection with Heaven?
- What do you want to do about that?

TODAY'S ACTION

What situation will you walk into today that has the potential to derail your connection with Heavens' priorities and perspective? Ask God what He wants to do in that situation. Now make a plan for how you will protect Heaven's priority.

Do you need to change who will be in the room? Would it help to set aside some time beforehand to focus? How else could you remind yourself of what is most important? Remember this is not a pass/fail but an opportunity to grow . . .

For more on this topic, see Bill Johnson's book, *Hosting the Presence*.

Twenty Two

DIVINE CONNECTIONS ARE WAITING FOR YOU

I remember the first-ever Dream Culture workshop we did. We had been talking about people living out the dreams of their hearts—the things that felt they were born for. As we asked people to stand and share one of their dreams, a man stood up and said, "I come from the East Coast branch of a national organization. I feel like God is showing me that I am to introduce the Holy Spirit into that same organization here on the West Coast. The challenge is I have no connections here with that group." Instantly a hand in another part of the room shot up and a lady asked if she could share something. We agreed and she stood to her feet saying, "I am a part of that organization here on the West Coast and not only that, I am good friends with one of the key leaders. Recently, he came to me and shared he was looking for ways to increase the influence of the Holy Spirit. I can introduce you." In one moment, what had seemed impossible became logical because God had *already* put the right people in the room.

Over and over again, we have seen the same thing happen. God seems to delight in orchestrating Divine connections where what we need is waiting for us in the life of a stranger on the other side of the room. I have a long history of seemingly stumbling into all sorts of connections with the right people at the perfect time.

Once I was at the Redding airport on my way to the UK. I had a connecting flight through San Francisco. I went through security and stood in the only waiting area, suddenly realizing I had left my phone back at the X-ray machine. I walked back and asked the security people but it was not there. As I was standing there wondering what to do, a female stranger beside me handed me her phone and said to call my number to see who picked it up from their possessions. I dialed and walked around the small area but no one responded. Next, the stranger lady walked around calling out loudly for people to check their phones because mine had been picked up by mistake. I felt like my mom had just walked in and taken over. But no one responded. We ended up boarding the plane still with no phone. I sat in my seat but the stranger lady was not one to give up so soon. She walked up and down the aisle of the small plane, dialing my number and asking people to check their phones. I was cringing thinking, "Mom . . . just sit down." Next thing the older lady beside me reached down into her purse and pulled out . . . . . my phone! I waved it in the air thinking, "Thanks mom!" with smiles all around. We relaxed ready to depart but then the captain came over the intercom saying we had to disembark because of mechanical problems. Well, at least I had my phone! Standing back in the lounge wondering how long the wait would be, I suddenly received a text. It was from the stranger lady saying, "Hey Andy, I don't want to wait and risk missing my connection so I've called for *my* plane. Do you want a ride?" What??!! I lost my phone and ended up with a private plane ride, courtesy of a stranger. What kind of favor is that?! The point is, God has always been in the business of putting the right people in the right place at the right time. He could have taken care of the situation Himself (and it would have been less messy), but He chooses to work through people time and time again. He involves us!

Look at these examples from Acts where God connects people for His purposes.

God gave Cornelius instructions to find Simon Peter.
Now send men to Joppa and send for Simon whose name is Peter.
Acts 10:5

Then God gave Peter instructions on how to find Cornelius.
Arise therefore, go down and go with them, doubting nothing; for I have sent them."
Then Peter went down to the men who had been sent to him from Cornelius and said,
"Yes, I am he whom you seek. For what reason have you come?"
And they said, "Cornelius the centurion, a just man, one who fears God and has a good reputation among all the nation of the Jews, was Divinely instructed by a holy angel to summon you to his house, and to hear words from you."
Acts 10:20-22

Then there is the story of God connecting Saul and Ananias:
Arise and go into the city and you will be told what you must do.
Acts 9:6

But the Lord said to him, "Go for he is a chosen vessel of mine to bear My name before Gentiles . . .
Acts 9:15

The connections in the verses above were critical in the lives of the people concerned. Cornelius gathered a crowd of Gentiles together as he waited for Peter to arrive. Peter had just had a vision about nothing being unclean (excluded), and suddenly he was thrust before Gentiles, who according to the Jewish religion, he was not even allowed to associate with. The meeting resulted in the entire group being saved and baptized with the Holy Spirit and this act opened the way for Gentiles around the world. Likewise, Saul had his sight restored when he met Ananias and began his ministry that ended up with him writing most of the New Testament. A couple thousand years later, I am sure you and I are both exceedingly grateful for both of those Divine connections and the resulting New Testament and salvation experience we get to access!

God wants to connect you with the right people that you need to propel you forward in your journey. Sometimes He is going to give you directions on where to find them. Sometimes it will seem like a coincidence that you just happen to bump into a certain person at a certain time. Sometimes the Divine connection is someone you would never have thought of asking for help or even being associated with. The key to finding Divine connections is asking God for them and then building an expectation that they are going to happen.

I started working for Danny Silk because of a Divine connection. A mutual friend introduced us at first, but that meeting was awkward, with neither of us really knowing what we were doing in the room together—we had completely different life stories. However, four months later as I finished my first year at the Bethel School of Supernatural Ministry, I thought I heard God tell me to talk to Danny about a possible internship. This wasn't part of the normal school process and I couldn't wrap my mind around any reason why this made sense, because of our differences—my business background compared to Danny's family life pastoring. Was I supposed to learn counseling???? Please no! However, I reached out with an email asking if he would meet to discuss the possibility of interning. At least I was being obedient. But God! After meeting and hearing a second time what I had been doing previously in New Zealand, Danny responded with, "You are an answer to prayer; when can you start?"

A simple Divine connection led to meeting Danny. That led to starting Dream Culture and writing our first book of the same name. Ultimately, it created the space for me to start what I am doing now—leading Heaven in Business and influencing people all over the world to experience God at work. It didn't look like an obvious connection at the start, but in hindsight, it was a Divinely orchestrated moment that changed both our lives. We don't always know why certain connections happen, and we certainly don't know what the long-term outcomes may be, but trusting that God can and does orchestrate the right connections for our future is the key to experiencing the future He designed.

PRAYER

Thank You, Father, that You are the Great Connector! Thank You that You put people in my path that connected me with You. I am here today because of the greatest Divine Connection—You. Thank you that You are have placed things inside of me to benefit others, and things inside of others to benefit me. Thank You that You are setting us up to succeed.

I ask You to bring the right people for this season into my life. Give me eyes to see the ones that You are giving to me as a gift. And help me to value every person that comes across my path.

GOING DEEPER

- What sort of Divine connection do you need right now?
- How are you willing to look beyond who you think is qualified for what you need?
- When have you seen God connect you in the past? What was the result? Let the testimony of how God has done it in the past give you hope for the future.

TODAY'S ACTION

Make a list of all the Divine connections you have already experienced that have gotten you to where you are today. Thank God for them. Now, intentionally go through your day looking for how you can help people around you gain access to the next step in their lives.

For further help in how to help people's dreams come true, read *Dream Culture: Bringing Dreams to Life*.

Twenty Three

BEWARE: COMPARISON KILLS YOUR BREAKTHROUGH

My wife and I run a ministry called Dream Culture and I lead Heaven in Business. Both ministries are designed to help people succeed and go further than they thought possible in their connection with God and in the things they put their hands to. As we have worked with people, we have seen many, many breakthroughs. One Managing Director of a large company flew out to a conference and the first morning received reports of a series of financial problems back at the business. Normally he would go into hyper-drive trying to fix everything. However, in this instance, he intentionally chose to experiment. He turned his heart and affection on God for the morning sessions and watched to see what God might do on his behalf (see Isaiah 64:4). As the session ended, he turned his phone back on to find two texts and an email saying the problems were more than taken care of in surprising ways. It was wonderful to see God fix his problems but at the same time we had our own personal problems that we could have used God's attention on fixing!

Over the years we have watched as the people around us have been outrageously blessed, often as a direct result (at least on the surface) of coming into contact with the work we do. There have been financial breakthroughs galore, some of them large sums of money. One friend received a car even as we were needing a new one. People around us were promoted and honored even as we served in silence. One person took what we trained him in and immediately started earning significantly more than we did, doing the same thing. At every turn we had the opportunity to compare and become envious. Some days it was really difficult to celebrate the people around us being promoted and blessed while we continued to wait. The very things we needed and desired were being given to the ones we helped. We loved that our work was causing others to prosper but we ached when they prospered in what we gave them, before we were experiencing it for ourselves. We had to make a choice on how to respond to the success of others even when we were in lack.

We learned that the fastest way to move away from the danger of comparison and envy is to celebrate others even more. We cheered loudly when they shared their good news. When we were able, we intentionally (and anonymously) sowed financially into their breakthrough 'tying' ourselves to their victory. We had to choose to avoid comparing ourselves with them because comparison is what feeds envy. We have learned to keep working and continue walking in our own lane, focusing on being faithful to what God has called us to do.

> *But when the Jews saw the multitudes,*
> *they were filled with envy; and contradicting and blaspheming,*
> *they opposed the things spoken by Paul.*
>
> *And the word of the Lord was being spread throughout all the region.*
> *But the Jews stirred up the devout and prominent women and the chief*
> *men of the city, Raised up persecution against Paul and Barnabas,*
> *and expelled them from their region.*
> *Acts 13:45, 49-50*

Paul was speaking the Word of God as he had been sent to do. The Jews heard the message first in the Synagogue and had a luke-warm response, but the gentiles were desperate to hear for themselves and begged Paul to tell them the same message. When the Jews saw the whole city responding to Paul, they became envious of what was going on and stirred up opposition against Paul, chasing him and his friends out of the region. The result was the Jews (and the city) missed out on the blessing that God intended through the hand of Paul.

Whenever we see someone doing better than us - greater influence, financial favor, or some other breakthrough- we always have a choice. Many people get envious and find a reason to talk about why that person doesn't really deserve what they just got. "Who do they think they are?" "Don't people know that they are arrogant and full of themselves?" "They probably manipulated their way into that result." In New Zealand we call this kind of behavior the 'tall poppy syndrome.' This is where when someone stands out above crowd, the crowd cuts them back down to average. Most people simply hold back on their gifting and capability because they fear being cut back down by the comparison and envy, and resultant nastiness of others.

It's the opposite in the Kingdom of God. His way is to celebrate the breakthrough and share in the joy of others. He goes so far as to say we should even love our enemies and pray for those who spitefully use us (see Matthew 5:44). We have to choose not to compare ourselves, our work, our service, our bodies, our children, our houses… anything.

I love mountain biking. One time I was in a leader meeting where one person shared how they had just taken up the sport and then been given a brand new, high end bike. I felt jealous. Part of me started to react… "God, I gave up so much of this when we left New Zealand, how come you haven't done that for me?" I caught myself in the moment and intentionally turned my heart to authentically celebrate his victory as if it was my own. A couple months later I received a random text from a friend. It said "Hey, I'm getting a new bike, do you want my old one?" I assumed his old one would be a great second bike for my wife so we could ride together. Then he dropped it off. It was more than 4 times the value of my bike and was perfectly setup for the kind of cross country and downhill riding I love. Needless to say, my wife doesn't ride it… (and she is not envious!)

In the midst of waiting for our breakthrough, God is wanting to grow our character to be like Him. Part of this process is refusing to compare ourselves with others, and refusing to be envious. The very act of celebrating the victory or breakthrough of others protects us from comparison and prepares us to handle our own breakthrough with humility. It's not easy unless we put aside our own need for acclaim, or finances or whatever it is we may be waiting for in that moment.

PRAYER

Lord, help me to live from the Kingdom value of celebration rather than comparison. Help me put my own needs and desires aside so I can genuinely celebrate others' victory. Help me recognize envy in all its forms and refuse to partner with it. Let me never tear down others because I am jealous of them.

Help me grow in the character that would be able to handle great breakthrough and be unmoved. Thank You that You are growing me to display more of Your character and ways.

GOING DEEPER

• Where have you compared your results (or lack of them) to

others and found yourself becoming envious or jealous?
- How can you practically celebrate the breakthrough of someone who is walking in the success that you are longing for?
- What does God have to say about the person you are jealous of? What does He say about you?

TODAYS ACTION

- Think of three people who have recently had a breakthrough in an area that you are wanting breakthrough.
- Take some time to thank God for their success and ask Him to show you His perspective on their situation.
- Send them a congratulatory text or anonymous note/gift (if prudent) to intentionally celebrate their victory as if it were your own.

Twenty Four

GOD OWNS AND OCCUPIES YOUR NIGHT

For a long season I struggled at night. I always fell asleep quickly but would consistently wake around 3am and my brain would start working overtime, thinking about all the things that were just outside my control. How on earth was I going to make all this work? I'd think about all the things where I felt like I was failing - as a father and husband, as a leader, as a steward of our finances... I'd get agitated at all the problems that I was facing at work. I would think through conflict conversations from multiple angles until my stomach was doing gymnastics with the anxiety. My mind would focus on the problems and I could never seem to find a solution. Needless to say, those nights were not exactly life-giving. Why is it that everything always seems so much worse at night!?

And then there are those seasons where even the daytime seemed like the night. Where everything around me seemed dark and foreboding, where hope was a scarce commodity and anxiety was around every corner. Where was God when I needed Him most? Where was He when I faced my darkest hour?

So many of us have experienced the long hours of lying awake wrestling with anxiety, fear and frustration. Or worse yet, we walk through seasons where the pressures are so significant that even the day seems like darkness. The darkness becomes a torment to us. We dread it, or we medicate it.

Then I bumped into a friend, Faith Blatchford, who just happened to be writing a book on sleep. It's called Winning the Battle for the Night. We had a quick talk then she gave me a draft copy. By the end of the first chapter my beliefs around night, sleep and darkness were blown apart.

In the beginning God created the heavens and the earth.
The earth was without form, and void;
and darkness was on the face of the deep.
And the Spirit of God was hovering over the face of the waters.
Then God said, "Let there be light"; and there was light.
And God saw the light, that it was good;
and God divided the light from the darkness.
God called the light Day, and the darkness He called Night.
So the evening and the morning were the first day.
Genesis 1:1-5

As God was creating the world, everything was dark and the Spirit of God was hovering, in the darkness, over the waters. God was inhabiting the darkness! He was brooding, creating IN the darkness. God was there BEFORE there was light. From the place of darkness He created. So creativity hovers in the night! God named the darkness night. So God owns the night! That changes EVERYTHING about what I believed about night and darkness.

God was there before the light; He inhabits the darkness. He is not afraid to dwell there. He owns it. He creates in it! And He wants to meet with us in the darkness. There is no darkness so dark that He cannot meet us there. There is no darkness that scares Him.

I started going to bed at night thanking God that He inhabited my night. I waited for the light to turn off and would lie there looking at the darkness and becoming aware that God was with me in the night. I would breathe in deeply thanking Him that He is my very breath. I would put on audio version of Psalms so that my last waking moment was listening to His Word.

I started to find other scriptures like:

> *You have tested my heart;*
> *You have visited me in the night;*
> *You have tried me and found nothing;*
> *I have purposed that my mouth shall not transgress.*
> *Psalms 17:3*

> *How precious are your thoughts towards me, O God!*
> *How great is the sum of them!*
> *If I should count them, they would be more in number than the sand;*
> *When I awake, I am still with You.*
> *Psalms 39:18*

God inhabits the night. God visits us in the night. He instructs us in the night. He speaks to us through night dreams. When we wake (or WHENEVER we wake), we are still with Him and Him with us.

That changes everything.

It was in darkness that Gods creativity was first unleashed. Is it possible that instead of dreading the darkness, He wants us to own it, and find

Him there? Is it possible that the night is the very time that He wants to unleash creative solutions to the problems we are facing – if we will get rid of the lies that stop us?

So what stops us finding God in the darkness? What makes the night seems so long and so devoid of hope? I believe that we find the darkness challenging in part because we feel alone. Whether the darkness of the physical night, or the darkness of a rough season, it seems like we are the only one that is struggling, wrestling with our challenges. Everyone is sleeping and we are the only one who has the thoughts that we have. Instead we must begin to consciously focus on the fact that we are not alone, that He is with us. When the enemy tries to convince us that we are alone in the struggle we need to begin to draw the Presence of the Father around us. We need to remind ourselves of those that God has put in our lives that do love us.

The other thing that makes the darkness hard is that we are often not thinking straight and we don't even know it. Our brains are only functioning at a certain level and we are definitely not operating at our best. We try and take on our hardest problems when we are at our worst and then wonder why we can't conquer them. And in the dark, we more often than not partner with fear. Fear is the enemy of creativity. The more we try to figure things out on our own and can't, the worse the fear gets. It's a downward spiral.

So, what is the solution? Cultivate the truth, knowing that He is with you. He is in the darkness just waiting to bring His presence and peace to you. Breathe deeply and become conscious of His Presence. Reject fear and embrace peace. Actively reject the influence of fear over your thinking. Tell yourself you will not think on these (difficult) things until the morning. Thank Him for His Presence with you in the darkness. If everything feels out of control, release all the pieces of your life that you can't control into His hands. He will meet you in the darkness, if only you will choose to find Him there.

I started waking in the night and instead of allowing myself to think on the challenges, I would quietly put in ear buds and listen to Bible on audio until His Words were louder than my thoughts. I would sometimes listen to worship music or recorded prophetic words, but mostly it was purely and simply scripture. I'd set the sleep timer to 30 minutes and very rarely be awake to notice that it had stopped.

God owns your night. Rest knowing that while you are sleeping He is Present, and creating all around you. Peace to your night!

PRAYER

Thank You, God, that You are in my darkness. Thank You that there is nothing to fear when You are with me. Thank You, that though my life feels out of control, You are leading me and You will never leave me alone. God, help me see the night as you see it. Let it be a daily time of encountering more of You. As I turn my affection to You and become aware of Your Presence, I ask You to meet with me and make me more like You. I invite You to inhabit my night.

GOING DEEPER

- What lies have you believed about sleep, the night and darkness? What is the truth God is speaking to you right now?
- How will you remind yourself that God is with you as you find yourself awake in the night, or walking through a dark season?
- Mediate on the truth that God's Presence is hovering over you, in the darkness while you sleep. What difference does make to how you feel about sleep?

TODAY'S ACTION

Talk to someone today about your what you are learning about God owning, inhabiting and creating in the night. Keep one another accountable in trusting God to inhabit the darkness each night before you go to sleep. Grab a journal and record each morning how you slept, what you did if you woke up and the first thoughts you had in the morning. Review this with one another.

Consider having communion each evening just before going to bed. This can simply be a cracker and water and remembering the covenant with Jesus who broke the power of every curse and all shame. You have complete victory because of the cross and His resurrection. Thank Him that his blood redeems the night and gives you the right to sleep in peace.

For more on this topic, see *Winning the Battle for the Night* by Faith Blatchford.

Twenty Five

REJECTION: YOUR PATHWAY TO LEADERSHIP

Our daughter Emily is a born leader. She is strong minded and very outspoken. She knows what she wants and is ready to pay the price to go after it. She is mature and responsible and hardworking. At age 17 she has already been leading in one environment for five years and is constantly having opportunities to lead in others.

As a parent though, we have had to watch as Emily has navigated rejection by her peers. Her teachers have often told us that she is wise beyond her years and that means, at times, she just doesn't fit it. On top of that, her core value of integrity means she won't compromise on what she believes even if it makes her unpopular. It is hard to watch her go through these hard times and at the same time we can see what is being strengthened in her as a result. She has developed a whole new level of perseverance. She has had to dig deep to find out who she really is and what she truly believes. The very journey of being rejected is what is preparing her for the life she will step into.

> *This Moses whom they rejected, saying 'Who made you a ruler and a judge?' is the one God sent to be a ruler and a deliverer by the hand of the angel who appeared to him in the bush.*
> *Acts 7:35*

As Moses finally stepped up at age 40, and engaged in his calling to lead his people he was immediately rejected. His efforts to step in and protect were misunderstood and the result was he had to run for his life. What he didn't know at the time, was the place where he ran to was the perfect preparation for where he was going to lead the people through. He didn't do anything wrong to be rejected by his own people. It was part of God's plan to develop him.

Likewise, Jesus was rejected, as was prophesied in the Psalms.

> *The stone which the builders rejected*
> *Has become the chief cornerstone.*
> *Psalms 118:22*

Jesus only did what He saw the Father doing. He went about healing the sick and doing good yet He was rejected and ultimately crucified by the very people He came to help. Sometimes we are rejected because we've done something to deserve it. But many times it is all part of God's strategic leadership development plan. Does He bring hard times upon us? No, but He sure will use those hard times to refine us. There are some things that can only be developed when we are alone in the wilderness. It is here we get to deeply reflect on what is most important to us and whether we will pay the ultimate price for what we believe in. Rejection is a normal part of the process being developed into a greater person of influence.

When we started Heaven in Business I thought everyone would jump on board. The opposite happened. Some of the people I thought would be most vocal and supportive, questioned what we were doing and why we were doing it. At one point I was told directly, "This is not going to work." Another time someone questioned whether it should continue at all. If this were strangers or people far away from me then I wouldn't care, but it was people close to me and whose opinions I held in high regard. Ouch. It hurt. I felt alone. But what it did do was force me to go deeper with God and really check in on what He said. The season wasn't fun but in hindsight was a NECESSARY GIFT that refined in me a strength of character that is critical if I am going to lead something significant. I needed to grow in courage. I needed to grow in perseverance. I needed to grow in my reliance on what God said rather than the approval of people around me.

I also needed to learn to partner with Holy Spirit for comfort rather than a spirit of rejection which is a false form of self-protection. When we are hurt we want to protect ourselves. True protection only comes from the Holy Spirit. Partnering with a spirit of rejection results in behavior that pushes away the ones that hurt you and goes even further to attempt to justify why you can keep your distance. This starts with saying things like, "I didn't really need or want that support/connection anyway." Inside it is saying, "I reject you for rejecting me" and results in setting up an invisible repellent to connecting with or influencing those people. If left alone, rejection grows to start pointing out the wrong in those people until you have completely justified why they are evil, you are good, and why you can stay at a distance from them. It is simply not the way of Christ.

If we stay humble and lean in to what God is trying to teach us when we are rejected, then He will turn the hard time into something beautiful inside of us. Jesus modeled this best when, nailed to the cross by the very ones He came to serve, He prayed, "Father forgive them for they do not know what they do" (see Luke 23:34). He kept his heart open towards those who rejected Him and trusted God to be His defender and redeemer. You and I are the result of that story.

I had to repent where I had partnered with rejection in pushing away people who had hurt me. This simply looked like praying out loud asking Jesus for forgiveness for the agreement I had made, acknowledging the pain I truly felt, and inviting Holy Spirit to be my only source of comfort and protection. The crazy outcome was that just days later, the very people that originally rejected me (years prior), invited me into places of support and influence that I wanted in the beginning.

Thanks be to God for His indescribable gift!

PRAYER

Jesus thank You for showing me the path of life. Thank You that You modeled the way we are to lead and love. Help me find You in the midst of rejection allowing it to refine my character like Yours. Help me stay humble and learning rather than getting bitter and offended. Forgive me where I have partnered with rejection to protect myself from hurt.

I invite Holy Spirit to be my only comfort and refuse to partner with offense. I bless those who hurt me and forgive them where they hurt me. Thank You for leading me into all truth.

GOING DEEPER

- Where have you experienced rejection? How did you respond?
- What was/is God wanting to develop in you through this season?

- What could you learn in this situation that you could never learn elsewhere? Ask God what He wants you to know at this time.

TODAY'S ACTION

Decide today to refuse any agreement with rejection and instead invite Holy Spirit to be your comforter in the midst of hurt.

- Tell Him how you felt.
- Forgive those who rejected you, releasing them from all expectation and obligation.
- Now ask Holy Spirit for one simple step you could take to move towards the ones who rejected you.

Twenty Six

WHO ARE YOU GOING TO PLEASE?

It was a bad night! Those same old feelings were back. I felt jumpy, my sleep was broken with not fun dreams and the wind was making the house creak in all sorts of weird ways. I lay awake worrying, questioning what I was doing wrong. Am I not working hard enough? Not exercising enough? Am I drinking too much coffee? Eating too much sugar? Am I not managing my time well enough? Am I trying to please too many other people?

As I lay awake again, I could feel the pull of the demands of others. I felt rushed and pressured by all the little things that needed to get taken care of and I kept getting interrupted by people with questions and problems that they wanted solved. Argh! There is just no way to make it all work, to answer all the questions, to make everybody happy with me. I had to come to the realization that I will never please everyone in my inner circle. I had to decide who I was going to please.

Will the Lord be pleased with thousands of rams,
Ten thousand rivers oil?
Shall I give my first born for my transgression,

The Fruit of my body for the sin of my soul?
He has shown you, O man, what is good;
And what does the Lord require of you
But to do justly,
To love mercy,
And to walk humbly with your God?
Micah 6:7-8

But let all those rejoice who put their trust in You;
Let them shout for joy, because you defend them;
Let those also who love your name
Be joyful in You.
For You, O lord, will bless the righteous;
With favor You will surround him as with a shield.
Psalms 5:11-12

I love how, in the first passage, the Psalmist asks "Do you need thousands of rams and ten thousand rivers of oil for me to please you?" It's an amount that seems so overwhelming as to be impossible. And then he says, "Well how about my first born, the most precious thing I can think of?" And then there is the conclusion of what God actually wants from us, to do justly, love mercy and walk humbly with our God. It's not about huge sacrifices or doing more. It's not about checking off everything on my to-do list or running about trying to please everyone around me. If I will just decide that today I will please God then the other demands around me pale in comparison. When I choose to trust Him, to delight in Him, then the rest will fall in to place.

When we choose to walk humbly with Him, our decisions and priorities get aligned with His priorities. Humility is not about running around serving everyone because we think nothing of ourselves. Jesus had a very clear sense of purpose and stayed within that. He had to say 'no' to many opportunities and many needs because He was humbly walking in what God had called Him to do. Jesus disappointed many, people, because He did not fulfill their expectations of Him. He still disappoints people today for the same reason. When we choose to please Him above all else, we will have awkward conversations and say 'no' to some people. We will disappoint people and delay their agenda (for us). It's not that we arrogantly ignore them, it is simply the fact that we cannot please everyone and one thing is important – pleasing Him.

When I start each day with the question, "What do I need to do today to walk in your pleasure?" then the pressures of others don't push in on me the same. When I order my priorities in light of His priorities, then it is easier to say 'no' to the things that aren't on His agenda for the day. I haven't got this down perfectly yet, but I am learning to not be moved by the needs and priorities of everything around me in order to live in a way that simply pleases Him.

The other thing I am learning is that if I DON'T get this sorted now, I am only transferring a bigger problem into my future. I have noticed that as I am faithful with my responsibilities and the people around me today, the favor and influence grows. With the growth comes MORE responsibility and MORE influence. This means more people pulling on what I can do for them. If I cannot decide and protect who I will please today, then tomorrow it will be an even bigger problem! I choose today to please God first. I prioritize my connection with Him and then from His perspective all other decisions fall into place. I will disappoint people; that is inevitable. But my significance and security are pre-established in His Presence. My future is going to be good!

PRAYER

Father forgive me for being pulled in so many directions by pleasing others. I still my heart and set my focus and affection on You first.

Thank You that Your love for me is unconditional and without regret. Help me feel Your pleasure on my life. Show me your priorities for me today. Help me to order my day with what is right.

Let me find my significance and security in Your Presence alone. Help me to simply do what's right, choose mercy and walk humbly with You. Always.

GOING DEEPER

- What pressures and demands are you facing from the people around you right now? What is God asking of you today?
- How will you prioritize connecting and seeking God's pleasure FIRST?
- How does knowing He is already pleased with you impact the way you see order other priorities?

TODAY'S ACTION

Take some time to be still, expressing gratitude and affection for God's goodness toward you. Once your thoughts have quietened, ask Him what His priorities are for you today. Write those down.

At the end of your day reflect on what happened. Ask Him how He feels about what you have accomplished (and not accomplished).

Twenty Seven

GET UP AND FIGHT!

The metaphor or image I have for my life right now is that of the US Navy at Pearl Harbor in 1941. I am in a fight for my life and that of my people. We just got bombed. It was meant to destroy us. We are not destroyed but we are deeply hurting. There are dead and dying people around me. There are delays and miscommunication and blaming. There is a real conflict going on and the casualties are real.

But I can't quit. I have too much invested with those I love. Anyway, where would I go? So, where is God in all of this? How do I survive? How do I fight? How do I lead? HELP!

It is amazing how God sets us up with what we need when we most need it. In the middle of feeling like I was in the fight of my life I happened to listen to a message from Pastor Bill Johnson. It was exactly what I needed. I realized I had allowed the size of the problem to become bigger than God Himself. As a result, I had become passive and powerless. I needed to stand up again. What I heard and experienced in that message gave me the strength and direction to do just what was needed - to remember the promises and fight with what God has said. This is when we discover the true value of worship, daily scripture (especially the Psalms), praying in the Spirit, declaration and remembering what

God has said. All of these daily Christian disciplines set our focus on God and keep us aware of how much bigger He is than anything else that would seek to say otherwise.

God only leads us through a conflict or challenge He knows we have the capacity to handle. Even more than that, God will strengthen us ahead of time and then set up opportunities to help us discover our authority – how much stronger we are than our enemy.

> *Israel also came into Egypt, And Jacob dwelt in the land of Ham.*
> *He increased His people greatly, And made them stronger than their enemies. He turned their heart to hate His people,*
> *To deal craftily with His servants. ...*
>
> *He also brought them out with silver and gold,*
> *And [there was] none feeble among His tribes.*
> *Egypt was glad when they departed,*
> *For the fear of them had fallen upon them.*
> *Psalms 105: 23-25, 37-38*

Throughout life God is training us and making us stronger. But training for battle is very different than battle itself. We have to have a fight in order to realize our authority. When God sees we are ready for the real thing, He goes over to the enemy and slaps them around and turns their hearts against us saying "It was their fault!" Next thing we find ourselves in a battle wondering what on earth happened and often questioning what we did wrong! But from God's perspective, it's already a foregone conclusion; it's a conspiracy to prove we are everything God says we are. It is also necessary for us to realize the authority that we have and to step into the future that He has for us. And the greater the battle the greater the reward.

But we will certainly need to know how to fight. And fighting God's battles is very different to earthly battles. First, we must remember that we are not fighting against people. People are not our enemy; the principalities and powers behind them are. The other big battle is in our mind – the head trash, mindsets and lies we believe that hold us back from stepping into all that God says about us.

> *For we do not wrestle against flesh and blood,*
> *but against principalities, against powers,*
> *against the rulers of the darkness of this age,*
> *against spiritual [hosts] of wickedness in the heavenly [places].*
> *Ephesians 6:12*

So how do we fight? The kingdom advances in two seemingly contradictory ways. The first way is by receiving like a child (see Mark 10:15). We cannot enter the Kingdom unless we come like a child. This is all about identity. We are children of God and our victory is not about our performance, it is about His – what He paid for. We receive everything Jesus paid for in full and we stand and receive what He has already done for us. We receive freedom and healing and provision and safety… the list goes on.

The second way to fight is a violent expression of faith advancing (see Matthew 11:12). This is all about understanding our position of authority. All authority was given to Jesus – meaning the devil has none. Jesus then gave all authority to us. We truly learn our authority as we exercise it. Through faith we take hold of things that are under the control of demonic influences and we forcefully advance the kingdom of God. We advance in freedom and healing and provision and safety.

When we have a promise from God and we are not experiencing the Kingdom advancing around us, we need to first ask Holy Spirit which way He wants us to fight. Do we simply receive and rest in what He has done or do we need to exercise our authority and fight? For me in this instance, I had become passive and was not experiencing any advancement; I needed to fight!

So I did. I started intentionally worshiping and praying in the Spirit daily. I started declaring what God had said over the situation. I reviewed what He had promised and turned that into a declaration in the middle of being surrounded by the opposite:

I am faced with financial challenges and internal poverty thinking:

- But God has said we have more than enough and more on the way!
- But God has said we will have land in this land!
- But God has said now is the time for every word to be fulfilled!
- But God has said there is no more delay!

Our reaction to challenge must be a declaration of the promise: BUT GOD HAS SAID…!

PRAYER

Father, thank You for preparing me for every challenge I face. Thank you for giving me opportunities to grow in authority. Help me to remember that You are always with me. Help me to stand up and fight in the way You are leading. Help me to remember Your promises toward me. Help me to remember the fight is spiritual not against people. Let me feel Your strength and power as I stand in who You have called me to be.

GOING DEEPER

- Ask God how much He has already prepared you strengthened for this fight. Ask Him how much authority He has given you over sickness and poverty. Ask Him how He has positioned you to win and what winning looks like?
- If you fully believed you are who God says you are and you have what it takes, how would that change your behavior in your current season? What would you do differently?
- What are the words and promises God has already spoken to you that you need to pick up and fight with now?

TODAY'S ACTION

Go back over the promises that you have heard from God, even as you have been working through this book. Turn them into a declaration in language that is directly opposite to the challenges you are facing right now. Write out the declaration(s) and put them somewhere prominent like your bathroom mirror so that you will read them daily. Take some time to stand and declare BUT GOD HAS SAID….

Twenty Eight

NO MORE COVER UP

I am a people person. If you are familiar with Clifton Strengths (Gallup), my top strength is Winning Others Over (WOO) and number three is Connectedness. My D.I.S.C natural behavioral style is 100% Influence. For seven years I worked as a Relationship Manager with an agricultural bank. All this means I am wired for relationship and while people respond quickly to trust me, I naturally avoid conflict or something that would seemingly undermine my connection. The bottom line is I tend towards procrastinating or straight out avoiding confrontation.

Add into this mix a religious upbringing that taught me what it means to be a "true" Christian. I must love others and love looks like forgiving and disregarding the offenses of others toward me. If someone hurts me, I should simply believe the best and move on:

> *And above all things have fervent love for one another,*
> *for "love will cover a multitude of sins."*
> *(Love forgives and disregards the offenses of others)*
> *1 Peter 4:8.*

Hatred stirs up strife, But love covers all sins.
Proverbs 10:12

Love suffers long [and] is kind;
love does not envy; love does not parade itself, is not puffed up;
does not behave rudely, does not seek its own, is not provoked, thinks
no evil; does not rejoice in iniquity, but rejoices in the truth;
bears all things, believes all things, hopes all things, endures all things.
Love never fails.
1 Corinthians 13:4-8

Growing up as I did and interpreting what these scriptures said about love, I had a biblical reason to cover over any hurt or offense and a legal justification for avoiding confrontation. I would just forgive the person who hurt or did me wrong and then stuff the pain... because love covers a multitude of wrongs.

So how did that work out for me?

Well after decades of 'legally' avoiding confrontation my wife kindly said to me one morning, "Andy, I will always love you, but you are dead emotionally toward me..." What!? Yes, I did hear correctly. I was being experienced as emotionally empty toward the one person that mattered the most to me. Ouch. This triggered a whole journey of unpacking how I dealt with pain and how I had been believing lies about what love does.

Every time I overlooked or covered an offense, it cost me a little piece of my heart. Over decades of this behavior, (plus other painful life experiences) I ended up with no heart left - an empty heart. Dead emotionally. I would do all that was necessary - physically being present for my wife and children, but I was not available emotionally. It is impossible to ignore or cover up a hurt without it costing us something. And what is more revealing is that when we have a vacuum in our heart, the first people to experience it are those closest to our heart – our spouse and family. The wider world around us has no idea that the core of our heart is dead emotionally.

And the scariest thing is I didn't even know myself!

Immediately after that conversation I was reading a book called The Business of Honor, about how an orphan's greatest fear is losing connection. This gave me a light bulb moment. I was behaving like an orphan, avoiding confrontation, because at my core I was afraid of losing connection!

I immediately repented for partnering with fear and asked Jesus to heal my heart and teach me how to protect it.

I then happened to have a conversation with Kris Vallotton as I wrestled with the scriptures about love covering everything. Were we not SUPPOSED to forgive and cover? Kris made a profound statement:

> "Andy, love covers a multitude of wrongs; but so does money, position and power."

Boom! Another light bulb switched on in my head. Throughout society I see this happening again and again. People avoid confronting or telling the truth because of money, position and power. And the underlying motive is fear! My fear was covering hurt and offense and I was calling it love. It was the greatest cover up and it was costing me my life! I looked into scripture some more and found what Jesus said about offense:

> *Moreover if your brother sins against you,*
> *go and tell him his fault between you and him alone.*
> *If he hears you, you have gained your brother.*
> *But if he will not hear, take with you one or two more,*

> that 'by the mouth of two or three witnesses every word may be established.' And if he refuses to hear them, tell it to the church.
> But if he refuses even to hear the church, let him be to you like a heathen and a tax collector."
> Matthew 18:15-16

Wow. Love doesn't just blindly cover a multitude of wrongs. Love actually confronts wrong doing, without cutting off or letting go of connection. Love embraces truth and cannot 'pretend.' True love see's the offense, acknowledges the offense, speaks to us about the offense and has no intention of letting go connection in the messy process. Now THAT is true covering. When I mess up, true love will confront me to help me see where I have made a mistake, without ever manipulating my response by withholding connection.

When we are hurt, we also need to learn how to protect and heal our heart. For this, we need to acknowledge the pain that wrong has done. Before we can forgive, we must know what we are forgiving people for. It's not just the pain in the moment, but also the ongoing effects that it has caused. Once we get to the depth of how much we have been affected, then we can truly forgive.

It's time to stop the cover-up and start speaking truth in love. And as much as it depends on us, hold onto our side of the connection.

PRAYER

Father forgive me for partnering with fear and avoiding confrontation. Forgive me for ignoring my heart and allowing myself to die on the inside. I receive Your grace and perfect love that chases away my fear. Thank you that I will never be lonely for You are near. I ask

You to heal my heart and restore my emotional capacity. Teach me how to protect my heart so I can love You and myself and others as You intended. Give me the wisdom and courage to speak the truth in love. I trust You to protect me.

GOING DEEPER

- Where are you avoiding confrontation or telling the truth because you are afraid of losing connection or damaging the relationship? What does that say about the depth of relationship?
- How alive is your heart? What would those closest to you say? What will you do about that?
- What is Jesus speaking to you about how much He loves you and how love operates?

TODAY'S ACTION

Who do you need to speak with about how they have hurt or done wrong to you? What will you do today to start speaking truth in love and trusting the outcome to God?

For more on this topic, read *The Business of Honor*, by Bob Hasson and *Keep Your Love On*, by Danny Silk.

Twenty Nine

MOVE FORWARD!

We had been walking through a wilderness experience for what seemed like years. Financially we were struggling and many areas of our lives seemed uncertain. Throughout the season we had been given words that God was going to provide a house for us but in the natural sense we were making no progress towards that dream. We had enough finances to get by but not enough to even save towards a deposit for a home. And still the prophetic words came of a promised home in the United States.

It was a terrific challenge to stay in a place of faith after so long of promises being given but seemingly not fulfilled. We got to the point where another prophetic word that mentioned a house was frustrating. We were grateful for the promise but we were ready for the cash! How do you keep trusting when the promise always seems just out of reach? And how do you respond when suddenly the waiting ends and you are faced with stepping into the promise and needing God to meet you there? As the time finally came for us to step into our breakthrough we had to choose to step in with great faith, not holding back, but moving forward with the conviction that God was with us.

The Lord our God spoke to us in Horeb, saying:
'You have dwelt long enough at this mountain.
Turn and take your journey, and go to the mountains of the Amorites,
to all the neighboring places in the plains, in the mountains and in the
lowland, as far as the great river, the River Euphrates.
See, I have set the land before you; go in and possess the land which
the Lord swore to your fathers – to Abraham, Isaac, and Jacob – to
give to them and their descendants after them.' 'May the Lord God of
your father make you a thousand times more numerous than you are,
and bless you as He has promised you!'
Deuteronomy 1: 6-8,11

The Israelites wandered in the desert for forty years because at the moment of breakthrough they didn't take God at His word. They had the promise of a land flowing with 'milk and honey.' God had told them He would give them the land. They had seen God work many miracles on their behalf, but as they reached the edge of the land they were promised, they were faced with a choice. Ten of the twelve spies that were sent out gave them a report of giants, the obstacles they would face if they crossed into the promised land. The other two spies told them of the beauty and benefits of the land and the fruit it contained. The people had a choice to make. They had heard the promises of God for years but now was the moment of breakthrough, and the moment of decision.

It's easy to look at the Israelites and think badly of them. How could they make such a dumb choice in the face of the goodness of God? Yet we do the same. I know that as we came to the edge of our 'promised land' (a house in our case) we were excited to step in, yet also fearful of the challenges that lay before us. We, like the Israelites, had to remember His goodness up to that point in order to move forward into the new territory. It was a lot bigger and scarier step than what we had rehearsed in our heads. In theory, possessing your promise is always simple and exciting, until you face the challenges IN your promise land that you must overcome in order to stay there.

Whenever you are moving into a new season you have a choice. You can look at the obstacles or you can gaze at His goodness and let that spur you on into the challenge of the new land. Great faith is essentially great risk. It was a risk for the Israelites to walk into the promised land. It was a risk for us to move into a new house, trusting God that He would give us the finances to support it. For us that looked like putting down a non-refundable deposit and renting for twelve months. We had no guarantee that we would have the funds at the end of that period. It was either going to be the most stupid, most expensive rental property in our lives, or it would be God. There was no in-between. We had so many promises and so much history with God providing that we had no excuse but to move forward.

It is time to walk forward confidently in the goodness of God. It is time to stop holding back. It is time to possess the land. It is time to hold up the banner of His goodness that you experienced in the past and let it speak to your future. Maybe your breakthrough is not yet visible, but nevertheless it is time to walk boldly towards it the best you know how, holding firm to the promises He has made to you. It is time to look the obstacles in the face and declare, "My God says you are mine!"

PRAYER

Lord help me to take you at your Word, no matter how long the journey has been. Let courage flood over me to boldly step into Your promises. Keep me from shrinking back when I see the challenges. Help me keep my focus on Your goodness and my history with You. Help me remember how you have led and provided for me every step of the way. Let me move forward with confidence!

GOING DEEPER

- What are the promises He has given to you that you can see are not far off?
- How does His goodness to you in the past speak to His faithfulness for your future?
- How will you boldly move forward into your breakthrough?

TODAY'S ACTION

What is one thing you can do today to partner with God and move forward? Don't hesitate, or overthink it. Just do it!

Thirty

PURSUE GOD FOR CONNECTION, NOT SURVIVAL

It's easy to prioritize spending time with God when we are in crazy times. When all of life seems to be crashing in on us and all we can see are the problems piling up, it's easy to turn to prayer. This kind of prayer sounds like "Help me, Jesus!!!" During our own crazy times, I have often laid awake at night overly aware of all the challenges I am facing. This has taught me to turn my thoughts toward Jesus, the Source of my strength and comfort. Practically, this usually looks like reaching for my phone, opening my audio Bible, plugging in my headphones, and listening to His Word until I drift off into sleep land.

More challenging, though, is keeping the same priority and passion for coming face-to-face with God when things are going well. When my wife and I first came to California, everything was uncertain. We had a visa status that had to be renewed each year. We had no income. And we would make friends only to have them move away as they completed their study at Bethel's Ministry School. It was a super challenging time. But it was also a time when we were almost forced into a nearness with God and rapidly grew as a result. The true driver to intimacy was mostly our external circumstances. As my wife put it, "In New Zealand, we stayed close to God because we chose to. Here, if I am not aware of His presence every day, I will be curled up in a fetal position in the closet."

Eventually, we secured permanent resident status in the USA, began to grow our income, and started to develop deep friendships with people who had made Redding their home. The intense uncertainty of the previous season came to a close and we felt great relief that we finally had some room to breathe! With this change came an awareness that we would have to intentionally respond to the pursuit of God in a different way than what had sustained us previously. No longer were we coming to God out our desperate need to survive; rather, it was a time to choose to be with Him face-to-face in a new way.

My beloved spoke, and said to me:
"Rise up, my love, my fair one,
And come away.
For lo, the winter is past,
The rain is over and gone.
The flowers appear on the earth;
The time of singing has come,
And the voice of the turtledove
Is heard in our land.
The fig tree puts forth her green figs,
And the vines with the tender grapes
Give a good smell.
Rise up, my love, my fair one,
And come away!
Song of Songs 2:10-13

The above passage is a phenomenal invitation from God Himself into a deeper connection. He paints a picture of the season change, when the flowers are blooming, the fruit is growing, a celebration is happening, and the joyful sound of birds can be heard. It is a picture of growth and beauty and joy. It is the season that we long for: flourishing in fruitfulness, beauty, and peace. But in this season, it is easy to be caught up in the productivity and joyful expansion and miss the invitation to come face-to-face with God in the midst of it. It is possible to be so caught up in the "miraculous" that our underlying relationship with God Himself is crowded out.

We must choose to respond to the invitation and come to an intimate place with Him. We must choose to draw away from the demands on our time, not because of crisis, but because of connection. There is a different way of relating to God when we are no longer in crisis. There is a heightened need to stay aware and grateful for all He has done, and for all He is to us. And just as we need to learn to change the way we relate to people as we go through different seasons, so we must learn to relate differently to God as we walk through different seasons.

As our season changed, we had to choose to prioritize hearing His voice every day, even though we didn't desperately need His direction to survive. I needed to restructure my priorities to protect the connection that was most important. I chose to put markers throughout my day to remind me to turn my heart and affection toward Him so that I didn't just get distracted with the good things that He had made possible. I took ownership of pursuing and learning to connect with Him in a new way. I am also aware that as I continue to walk and grow with God, there will be different seasons where the way I pursue and prioritize my connection with him will again need to change. I don't do this because I need His voice to survive a crazy time; I do it because I greatly value my connection with Him and I absolutely love hearing His voice.

PRAYER

Lord, let me always lean in close to You, in crazy times and especially in the good times. Cause my ears to be open to hear Your voice. Let me be aware of Your Presence with me. Help me to choose You over the busyness of life. I love You. Thank You that in all you could do, You choose to be with me.

GOING DEEPER

- What have you noticed about your connection with God when the season has changed?
- What does your current routine or schedule show about how important your connection with God is?
- Ask God how He feels about your connection with Him and what He is inviting you into.
- How could you prioritize and protect your connection with God?

TODAY'S ACTION

Make a plan and commitment to pursue and protect your connection with God when the season changes. Set up markers in your day to remind you to turn your heart and affection toward Him. This could look like an alarm, or calendar appointments, or visual reminders like a sign or picture somewhere in your work or home.

RECOMMENDED RESOURCES

Crucial Conversations – Tools for Talking When the Stakes are High, by Patterson, Genny et.al.

Daring Greatly – How the Courage to be Vulnerable Transforms the Way we Live, Love, Parent and Lead, by Brené Brown

Dream Culture – Bringing Dreams to Life, by Andy and Janine Mason

Good Morning Holy Spirit, by Benny Hinn.

God with You at Work, by Andy Mason

Hosting the Presence – Unveiling Heaven's Agenda, by Bill Johnson.

HeaveninBusiness.com – Blogs, events, advisory, online learning and like-minded community.

Keep Your Love On – Connection, Communication and Boundaries, by Danny Silk

The Business of Honor -Restoring the Heart of Business, by Bob Hasson and Danny Silk

Questions for Jesus – Conversational Prayer Around Your Deepest Desires, by Tony Stoltzfus

Winning the Battle for the Night – God's Plan for Sleep, Dreams and Revelation, by Faith Blatchford.

ABOUT THE AUTHOR

Andy Mason comes from New Zealand and has 15+ years of experience helping individuals and organizations discover and align with purpose, then develop practical steps to make dreams a reality. He has worked for a national consultancy firm and a leading financial institution and has invested in international community development. Andy is the founder and director of Heaven in Business (see HeaveninBusiness.com), a movement to connect and catalyze believers in the marketplace to partner with God in their realm of influence. This has led to the development of curriculum in Bethel's School of Supernatural Ministry, workshops and conferences, an online learning platform, and a growing community of men and women in the marketplace who are distinguished from their colleagues by the tangible Presence of God. Andy is the author of *God With You at Work*, available in multiple formats.

Together with his wife, Janine, Andy also leads *Dream Culture*, catalyzing people to discover and live their dreams. In 2011, they coauthored the book *Dream Culture: Bringing Dreams to Life*. Their Dream Journey workshops are now being used in churches, schools and community centers around the world.

Download and share free chapters and other resources from Andy and Janine at AndyandJanine.com/downloads

  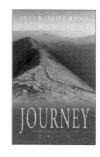 

THE HOPE DIRECTIVE

If you have found this resource helpful and want to multiply this and more for others, consider partnering with us through The Hope Directive.

The Hope Directive is a registered 501(c)(3) whose purpose is to ignite hope in individuals and organizations around the world. We do this by developing and distributing resources and presentations that equip people with hope towards a better future and by partnering with other like-minded organizations to do the same. The outcome is people and the teams they work with, aligned with purpose and vision and moving forward to make the world a better place for our children's children.

To find out more visit AndyandJanine.com/HopeDirective